A
MISDIAGNOSED
NATION

Donny,
God is moving in your life
brother and I am excited to
see what he will do in your life
God Bless
Steve

A
MISDIAGNOSED
NATION

Transforming America with an
Inwardly Sound &
Outwardly Focused Culture

STEVEN J. WILSON

EPILOGUE BY BRITTANY WILSON

Donny,
Never stop
pursuing your dreams
Blessings,
Britty Wilson

TATE PUBLISHING
AND ENTERPRISES, LLC

Published by Tate Publishing & Enterprises, LLC
127 E. Trade Center Terrace | Mustang, Oklahoma 73064 USA
1.888.361.9473 | www.tatepublishing.com

Tate Publishing is committed to excellence in the publishing industry. The company reflects the philosophy established by the founders, based on Psalm 68:11,
"The Lord gave the word and great was the company of those who published it."

Book design copyright © 2012 by Tate Publishing, LLC. All rights reserved.
Cover design by Kate Stearman
Interior design by Sarah Kirchen

Published in the United States of America

ISBN: 978-1-61862-970-8
1. Political Science/Commentary & Opinion
2. Social Science/General
12.05.17

GUEST CONTRIBUTORS

DON CARLSON

JODY ALLEN CROWE

TIM SPIKER

ACKNOWLEDGEMENTS

I would like to acknowledge my family for their endurance and patience during the time to write this book. To Jeanne, my wife, for accepting the responsibility of creating the endnotes. Any woman who is willing to do this for her husband has demonstrated her love like no other! To my son, Ben, for his wise counsel and creative input. To my daughter, Brittany, for dragging me to a writers' conference. Now here we are working on a book together!

I would like to also thank my guest contributors for their willingness and trust in this project: Don Carlson, who actually went through the work of providing new material for this book; Jody Allen Crowe, who took the time out of a hectic schedule to provide a summary version of his book; Tim Spiker and his wife, who recently had their second child, and we are celebrating with them! Tim has graciously provided permission to use the information from his website for use with this book.

Finally, to all the volunteers who provided their time and expertise to this project, thank you for being outwardly focused!

TABLE OF CONTENTS

INTRODUCTION

I had mentally prepared for some minor discomfort. I had no interest in going below the surface and stirring up any significant pain. After he finished the X-rays, my dentist came back with a surprising report. I needed a root canal. *No way! This is not the reason I came here today.* If I had been three years old, I would have thrown myself on the floor and yelled for Mama. But I was in my forties now, and I would have to act all grown-up-like.

So, what just happened? What happened was my dentist went from a surface situation to a root situation. He was simply going below the surface and checking for any root issues, and he found one. We see this every day in the medical industry. We go in for routine physicals, and, once in a while, our doctor may want to do an MRI and check for root issues. Our mechanic may want to go beyond that oil change and go inside the engine.

In the business world, we look for root issues. For example, sometimes we find a manager who lacks any natural ability to manage. In agriculture, we go below the surface and find things like root rot. In construction, we have issues with foundations and basements under a building.

Okay now, stop right there. Put the brakes on and come to a complete halt. We will now enter a new world: the world of social and political issues. As you look around, something has changed. In this sociopolitical world, we start to *avoid* the root issues. In this new world, we experience surface dwellers. There is a tendency to avoid or even deny the existence of root issues ... that is, until today.

This book will take you into those hidden places that receive little attention. We will introduce you to a whole world of root issues. We will walk into caves and discover we are only in the entrance, and there are many other caves attached to the back of the entrance. Hopefully you will find answers and perspectives never revealed before. I want this to be challenging and enjoyable at the same time.

The whole genesis of this book was spontaneous. I started waking up in the morning with ideas in my head, and soon I started jotting them down. Within a few days, I was seeing the possibility of a PowerPoint presentation evolving. Many of my life experiences were starting to come together like pieces of a puzzle. Dots were being connected. Have you ever had that happen? I've had it happen in small ways, but this time it was bigger. I kept adding on to my PowerPoint, and eventually I had to transition to word processing software.

Right in the middle of this adventure, an old friend named Gary, sent me a document I had written four years previously which I had totally forgotten even existed. I added it to my growing list of ideas and information. Within three months, I had enough words to comprise a book, and the next thing you know, I was looking for a publisher. I can honestly tell you writing a book was the last thing on my mind. So, what is happening to me?

The best way I can explain it is this: in the newest version of the movie *Karate Kid*, Will Smith's real-life son plays the part of a young preteen boy who is thrust into the Asian culture. In the beginning of the movie, something grabs his attention out of the blue. He runs across the street and yells back for his mother to follow. He breaks into a clearing that introduces him to a new world. It is the world of kung fu. What is his reaction? He is nearly mesmerized by everything he is seeing in front of him. Something about this new picture is resonating inside the *Karate Kid*.

There are many other movies that tell true stories of awestruck characters, such as future baseball players walking into a professional baseball stadium and being overtaken by the grandeur of the experience. At that moment in time, they have little experience and would not be able to make it to first base even if a slow pitch came their way. Despite the lack of training in all these situations, something has sparked inside these future players. They have identified a seed that is waiting to grow and make an impact. Maybe that can happen to old people, too. Maybe that same discovery can happen to middle-aged people. Maybe that's what is happening to me. Time will tell.

I realize social issues and especially political issues can put anyone to sleep in record time. I will do my best to share stories that will illuminate the points being made. I will take you on trips from the hills of the Midwest to the deserts of the Middle East. I will share childhood memories and lifelong victories. I will introduce you to farmers and four-star generals. I will introduce you to three guest contributors. With their help I have assembled three case studies to support my approach to root issues. I can almost guarantee that after reading this book, you will look at leaders differently. Instead of focusing on a person's nice hair, you will know what to look for in a truly effective leader. If you are looking for specific solutions to root issues, you will find them here. Near the end of the book I will provide a detailed political solution, a detailed social solution and one solution for you personally to participate in the transforming of our culture. Many authors will stay clear of the topic of faith as it might scare people away. We will respect that need for separation and will describe faith's influence on root issues in the final chapter. To wrap it all up we will even provide you with a fictional epilogue. Like many good books, we will start simple and then build to a pinnacle in the end. In this book, we start in the garden.

1

DIAGNOSING LIFE'S ISSUES

I had no idea that riding a Blackhawk helicopter would become routine. Ironically, boarding and exiting choppers had been overlooked in my training. Today was my first time in a Blackhawk as I flew from Baghdad south to Forward Operating Base Kalsu. I would land in an area between the Tigris and Euphrates rivers. Some would say this is the cradle of civilization. It was near the beginning of my one-year tour as a civilian diplomat embedded in the army in Iraq. I was assigned to the Fourth Brigade Combat Team of the Third Infantry Division and was traveling as a unit of one. I had no idea what would lie ahead as the *birds* landed at the base.

A thousand questions had gone through my mind since I had started the deployment paperwork with the U.S. State Department almost a year earlier. Would I adapt to the 120-degree heat while wearing forty-three pounds of tight fitting body armor? How much time would I spend in the Red Zone or frontline? Would I adapt to military life with absolutely no experience under my belt? Would I make any friends?

Today I would finally start to answer some of those questions of self-preservation. I was happy to find that someone greeted me shortly after arrival. It was my first supervisor. His name was Colonel Nye. This man was all military. If he saw potential in people, he was eager to take them under his wing and get them on their way.

In the first few weeks, he made a comment that stuck with me: "Being a patriot is neither comfortable nor convenient." What gives this statement deep meaning is that these words come from a man who was deployed away from home for most of the time period between 9/11 and 2008. Not only did he demonstrate tremendous commitment during the Iraq war as a *full-bird* colonel, but his service to our nation also dated back to the Vietnam War. Few could argue the fact that Colonel Nye was outwardly focused. He was a public servant and a patriot wrapped into one.

It was here in Iraq that I was able to experience true leaders all around. Everyone was a servant leader. Success was measured by what a person had on the inside. Being inwardly sound was not questioned. The bigger question and harsh reality was if you would still be inwardly sound when you went home. Everywhere I looked, self-discipline was a starting point, not an afterthought. It reminded me that without self-discipline, America would have only amounted to a pool of ideas. It was self-discipline that won every war and allowed the fourteen-plus trillion dollar economy we experience today. Remove self-discipline from the future, and we will gradually fade into the sunset as a pool of ideas, with another empire reaping the benefits.

What about this disciplined style of leadership? Is character really that crucial? Is being inwardly sound and outwardly focused important in leadership? Is self-discipline really that imperative when it comes to leaders? For me personally, I spent a year in a warzone experiencing all these character traits in leaders.

The next year was different, very different. The year after returning from Iraq, I ran for U.S. Congress. There is some deep contrast in what I experienced from one year to the next. I went from being embedded in the army to embedded in politics. The first year promoted self-discipline, and the next year seemed to reward the opposite. The environment I experienced the first year was about covering your neighbor's back, and the environment I experienced the second year was about stepping on your neighbor's back. The culture I experienced the first year embodied integrity and honor. The culture I experienced the second year, well, honestly, I don't even know how to articulate the difference except to say that there is an underlying darkness that permeates the political culture.

What I can tell you is that for forty-four years, the Harris Poll has measured how confident the American people are in the leaders of major U.S. institutions. The 2010 results showed the U.S. military with the highest confidence rating at 59 percent. Who had the lowest? The results in that same year showed the U.S. Congress had a confidence rating of 8 percent.[1] Yes, our U.S. Congress ranked at the bottom. Aside from the founding of our nation and the period of the Civil War, I believe there has never been a time when the nation needed a more thorough examination. What is going on at the core? What are the real root issues? That is the purpose of this book.

During our time together, we will focus as much on the process used to examine our nation as the examination itself. The process of examination or diagnosing is a big part of our nation's challenge. What do I mean by that? We focus most of our time and attention on what we see on the surface. We do not take the time to go below the surface and look at the root of our issues. If our nation were a patient getting a physical at the doctor's office, it would get a slap on the back and a piece of paper for a prescription that would cover the pain. After three refills of painkillers, it is time to look closer and go deeper.

Every day there are people in the news talking about surface issues in America. It is time to take an X-ray to find what is really causing the pain. In this book we will look at those X-rays, CAT scans, and MRIs. By the time you finish this book, it will be clear: we have a misdiagnosed nation.

Little did I know my first lesson in diagnosing life's issues would come when I was five years old.

"Make sure you pull them out by the roots!" I heard from across the garden.

I was not old enough to be working around the animals yet. As the youngest child on the farm, I was assigned the task of helping my mother pull weeds. From my vantage point, it seemed like two acres of weeds in one acre of garden. I had decided it was too much work to pull those stubborn weeds out by the roots, so I started to leave the roots and rip off the green part above the surface of the ground. I reasoned that, from a distance, my siblings walking by the garden would not be able to tell the difference, at least in the short run. What I had forgotten is that I was working with a trained professional right next to me. My mother could spot a weedless root a mile away and, worse yet, identify the person who left the root. My mother was not afraid to confront the root or the person who was unwilling to deal with the root.

"You will just have to come back and pull it up later," was a follow-up comment to me across the early morning air, reminding me that my solution was only temporary in nature.

Fast-forward forty years. My wife, kids, and I have just set out some big plants on our front porch before my mother came for a visit. We were admiring the beauty of the big, potted plants and the vibrant feel they gave to the front steps of our home. When my mother arrived, she walked up to the cedar porch, approached the plants, and plucked all the flowers off the plant, pruning it back to just the stems. My wife and I were both shocked. We gave each other a nervous smile and said nothing. We knew, however, my mother was a person with great self-discipline, and she was probably doing something good.

So what was different from what she was teaching me back at the farm? Let's look at this lesson in life issues as taught through the lens of a gardener. What was the difference in the plants in my home garden and the plants on our front porch? One plant was a weed, and one plant was a flower. How were they handled differently? The bad weeds got pulled out by the roots below the surface, and the good flowers were carefully pruned back above the surface. What was the difference in the outcome? The weeds that were pulled out by the roots died and no longer existed. The flowers that were pruned above the surface flourished with even more flowers than before the pruning.

The natural ability of the gardener is also noteworthy. My mother was not afraid of confronting the root beneath the weed. She was disciplined in a way that only the Great Depression could teach. Leaving the root was not even in her thought process. She had learned through the years that leaving the root intact and dealing only with the surface of the weed was futile and temporary at best.

Who would have thought some of the very secrets of life's issues and conflict management could be found in our own garden? Gardening and plant biology is not the only metaphorical indicator of root issues or beginning points. Geology points to bedrock as a beginning point of an earthquake. The construction arena can point to a cracked foundation when a house is unstable. A psychologist may ask about one's childhood when dealing with a troubled patient.

Does this same philosophy have an application or use in the social and political areas of our nation? In many of today's macro issues, we have transitioned to leaving the roots of weeds in the ground and not dealing with them. We do not have the discipline it takes to deal with the root issues of life. It is much less painful to talk about surface issues. Eventually, the average person without trained eyes will not even question the existence of a root. The untrained eye of the novice may not even notice the little stubble that is still sticking out from the root under the surface. Meanwhile, the person who comes up with a seemingly wonderful solution for treating a symptom or surface issue with temporary painkillers will score points for their list of overrated solutions.

What other areas do we learn about by diagnosing life using this root-issue philosophy? After leaving the farm, finishing college, and jumping into the corporate life, the idea of diagnosing root issues popped into my life again. I was privileged to work with a team of business consultants that would work with individual business owners who were clients of the corporation. Once a month, our team would conduct staff meetings consisting of consultants from around the Midwest and the eastern part of the nation. Our supervisor, Steve, would ask us questions during our reports that coached us on root issues.

"So, what is the real issue?" was the question we often heard.

We would think for a while and reply, "Well, it's a budget issue."

"Okay, what else? What about the budget?"

"Well, there is too much spending."

"Okay, why is there too much spending?"

"Well, the manager does not have the natural ability to manage."

Bingo. Now we are getting somewhere. What just happened? We dropped from surface issues to a root issue. My supervisor was an expert at working in the root issues. His second-favorite statement was "Let's get it on the table and deal with it."

Now we hear a lot of people using this phrase, but I think he was the one who invented it. For most people, getting a root issue on the table and dealing with it does not come naturally. It can be controversial in nature or at least perceived to be controversial. It can also be more painful to deal with than surface issues, or at least be perceived to be more painful. However, there can also be great rewards, as many of you can attest, when the root issue has been removed. The removal provides a longer-term resolution.

Once I had been trained to use the root-issue philosophy in business, I began to think about other areas of my life. What about conflict management? During a two-day seminar on conflict management, I approached the trainer during a break. We had been discussing resolution techniques, but it still did not seem to go deep enough. During the break, I asked the trainer, "What percent of people that express anger are doing so because of previous unresolved anger or from a lack of self-esteem?" I wanted to see if there was a prevalence of root issues in conflict management.

The trainer thought for a while and said, "Between 80 and 90 percent."

I found that fascinating. This continued my curiosity about root issues. My corporation was spending a lot of money to train staff to deal with people who have unresolved anger and low self-esteem. It would seem there should be a way of more effectively and efficiently dealing directly with the root issue. It seemed these unhappy personalities were the result of delayed responses to something deeper in their life. We will address delayed responses a bit more in chapter three.

The idea for this book came to me after running for U.S. Congress in 2010. I was an endorsed candidate with the Independence Party of Minnesota. My campaign had done extensive research on policy and provided ten solutions to our nation's pressing issues relative to the district I live in. Many of the people on my campaign felt like there was something out there that had yet to be articulated when it came to solving many of our nation's problems. Most of the solutions focused entirely on the surface issues. This book may not have all the answers, but I think the approach is better. The campaign trail did not seem like a warm, friendly place to discuss root issues. Five-second sound bites are not long enough. Hopefully this book will be a better venue. What counts in campaigns are negative advertising, good hair, and money. This explains very quickly why I did not win. I did not have any one of the three! Unfortunately, clean TV ads, short hair, and a thin pocketbook do not get you into office.

I believe the time has come for a discussion about root issues. Not only will you find this book a good resource for diagnosing our nation, it should also help you with your everyday life. You can start today, right now in chapter one, to think about recent problems in your life. Take some time right now to think about the root issues. Think about a situation that you struggle with or have struggled with in your past. Were you looking at it right? Or was there something below the surface you might not have seen before?

One day I was struggling personally with a migraine headache, and as the day went on, I was becoming more agitated with one particular problem. The more I thought about it, the more agitated I got. I'm sure you have those times yourself. I got to the point of making a phone call when I stopped and asked myself, "Wait a minute. What is the root issue here?"

Even just a few seconds of properly diagnosing my situation revealed that the migraine was the root issue. My next move reflected a better diagnosis. I chose to not make the phone call. I recognized the phone call would only deal with a surface issue. The next morning the headache was gone, and so was my anxiety over the problem. If I had made the phone call, I would not have been addressing the root issue, and I would have made a mess that would have only taken more time to clean up.

Before we move on to chapter two, let's summarize chapter one with this simple chart. It is important that we clearly distinguish between surface issues and root issues.

SURFACE ISSUE	ROOT ISSUE
More Visible	Less Visible
Less Perceived Pain to Resolve	More Perceived Pain to Resolve
Shorter Impact	Longer Impact

Secondly, let's summarize what we learned in the garden.

LESSONS FROM THE GARDEN

We can learn three things from a good gardener. First, a good gardener can spot a weed with the top pulled off (root issue) a mile away. Second, a good gardener is not afraid to confront the root or the people who left the root in the ground. Third, a good gardener makes sure their staff is well educated in the cost of leaving a root of a weed in the ground.

"You will just have to come back and pull it up later."

ROOT LESSON FROM CHAPTER ONE:

The garden and gardener
can teach us a lot about life.

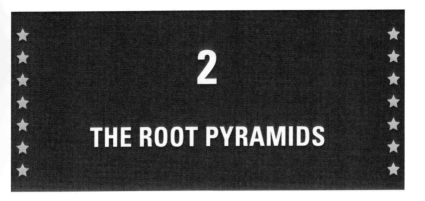

2
THE ROOT PYRAMIDS

As I looked into their eyes, it seemed as though something was missing. One by one, I interviewed workers in the Former Soviet bloc country of Hungary. Eastern Europe had just come out of decades of rule by a Communist takeover. Hungary was the first and, likely, the smoothest transition to democracy. In 1989, the Soviet Union signed an agreement with Hungary to withdraw Soviet forces by 1991. Changes came rapidly after 1991, and America was quick to provide support for this nation's new endeavors.

My small role in 1993 was to help the privatization of a former Soviet-run business. I was a consultant contracted by the United States Agency for International Development (U.S.AID). The specific business I was assisting had an excellent new manager. His name was Eshtvan. We were implementing new employee-management techniques, and he agreed to the idea of allowing employee participation in some of the new changes we were evaluating. This gave me a wonderful opportunity to interview dozens of employees. It became obvious after the first ten or so interviews of Hungarian workers that a pattern was developing. Something was missing in their eyes. It was hope.

Years of being servants to communist rule had affected their inner zeal for life. Living in meager conditions year after year with little hope for change had taken its toll on this country. A new tenant had occupied the space where hope had lived. It was apathy. This lifestyle of communist rule was the only thing most of them had ever experienced in their entire lifetime. In many ways they had given up on change, and there was little they could do about it. Yes, they were two years into a new country, but their job had not changed, and the new infrastructure had not yet solidified. It was still too early in the transition away from Communism to see daily conditions progressing to any great degree. As a matter of fact, some businesses were waiting six months to get paid for their product.

However, what I heard coming from the voices of those being interviewed was more encouraging. Despite the apathy in their eyes, their voices struggled to show some level of optimism. Optimism for the future would be a complete paradigm shift. Before their new Western-style democracy, the only thing they looked forward to in their lives over the long run was raising a family and in the short run having beer with their noon meal. At that moment on that day, however, the fact that they were being asked for their opinion in the workplace was entirely new to them and seemed to spark some curiosity into what might lie ahead. Maybe hope was still a possibility.

What was the genesis of this new independence? How did the transition start? It started with a change in root issues. The world had tolerated bad behavior from the former Soviet Union long enough. On June 12, 1987, President Ronald Reagan stood in front of the Berlin Wall and spoke those famous words, "Mr. Gorbachev, tear down this wall." In 1989, the Berlin Wall did come down, and in 1991, Mikhail Gorbachev resigned. A week later the Soviet Union was done. A lot had happened during these few years: the Iron Curtain fell, and nations like Hungary in Eastern Europe were free again.

The specific root issue that changed in the world was in the category of core values. Occupying other countries was a principle and core value that was not right. People should be free. Hungary was one of several countries that directly benefited from this solidifying of core values. Now it was up to Hungary. The ball was in their court. They finally had the chance to find resilience, change direction, and live up to their potential. Slow as it was, they were responding, and even though I was only there for a short time, it was exciting to see a nation work through their issues and become a sustainable nation. Since Hungary, I have had the opportunity in brief segments to see firsthand three other countries work through major issues on a national scale. I was in the Czech Republic doing similar work as in Hungary, in Honduras while they were recovering from a hurricane, and more recently in Iraq for a year during the war as an economic advisor.

In this chapter we will organize the root-issue philosophy and create a diagram to help us understand more about root issues. In chapter one, we used the garden as a source of our knowledge. We will do the same in this chapter and learn from nature. What can we learn from nature and science and then apply to everyday living? For this application, it would only seem appropriate to learn about root issues by studying what lies in the ground under the garden. College-level agriculture classes can spend an entire semester on the topic of soils. There are people who work as soil scientists by profession. One of the first and most basic things we learn in soils is something called soil horizons. A simplified soil horizon under the garden consists of bedrock at the bottom, subsoil in the middle, and top soil on top. Each soil horizon has similar characteristics and compositions. I will use a diagram in the shape of a pyramid to illustrate the soil horizon and call it a garden pyramid. Since this book focuses on root issues, we will not spend a lot of time analyzing the garden itself above ground. There are a lot of books already available that deal with the vegetables, so to speak, on top of the surface.

Here is what the garden pyramid looks like.

GARDEN PYRAMID

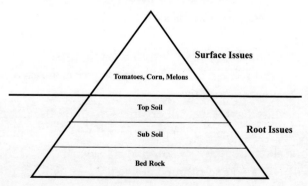

Now that we have a picture, we can identify the nature of the area underground. We will identify four characteristics about this pyramid and then compare this to a second pyramid later in the chapter called a Social and Political Pyramid. Here are the four characteristics of the garden pyramid:

Surface and Root

There are two basic areas in the garden pyramid. There is activity both above the ground and below the ground. A good gardener will analyze both areas. Certain plants will only grow well in certain soils. Appreciating the value of both surface and root issues will determine the success of the gardener.

Hierarchy

The surface issues do not seem to have hierarchy. There are no king vegetables. The root issues do seem to have hierarchy and order.

Root Order

The area underground, on the other hand, actually has order. There are categories that are easily identifiable.

1. Bedrock is the hardest to see, but the lack of visibility is not an indicator of significance. Bedrock has the ability to literally shake the earth if it is broken. It can cause mass destruction in minutes. Point being, there is a lot going on under the surface. Often we will forget that the bedrock even exists since it is the most difficult to see. We may not even recognize the need for bedrock or the value of bedrock. That comes

only when we build our house above a fault line or broken bedrock. Eventually, the result will likely be destruction.

2. Subsoil is above the bedrock. Subsoil can be broken down into a small number of layers within the subsoil. Long standing plants will grow roots down into good subsoil for a longer life.

3. Topsoil is above the subsoil. It is the most visible to humans. Topsoil works best when the subsoil and bedrock are stable and have not been altered by humans.

Root Dynamics

Changing the order of the layers does not work. What would happen if we switched bedrock and subsoil around? What would happen if the subsoil was on the bottom of the soil horizon and the subsoil was shifting sand? How stable would the ground be on the surface? Would it be a good place to build? Obviously not. There is a reason why bedrock is at the bottom and subsoil comes next.

SOCIAL AND POLITICAL PYRAMID

In this next section, we will use an analogy. We will use the garden to help us understand social and political principles. We will use the more tangible root issues of the garden to identify the less tangible character of social and political root issues. In other words, the two pyramids in this chapter have a lot in common. This brings us to the development of our second pyramid.

It is called the Social and Political Pyramid. Let's take a look at the same four characteristics from the garden pyramid.

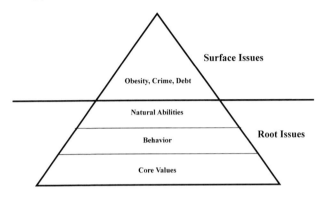

Surface and Root

There are two basic areas in the Social and Political Pyramid. There is activity both above the ground and below the ground. The top area represents surface issues, and the bottom area represents root issues. I have included three examples of surface issues. I would estimate there are an unending number of surface issues and a more quantifiable list of root issues.

Hierarchy

As we look closer at the dynamics of the pyramid, the surface issues do not have any type of hierarchy. All surface issues are on the same level. In other words, they can all be affected by the root issues below. However, the root issues appear to have a hierarchy in their structure.

Root Order

Root issues, like the garden, have more structure. I have identified three categories in the diagram that root issues may fall into. Even with the use of these categories, I will be quick to admit the approach is not black and white. Your experiences may reflect a different list of categories; however, we will start with core values, behavior, and natural abilities.

1. If bedrock is the base of the pyramid in the garden example, I would suggest that *core values* are at the base of the social and political pyramid. Core values are just that. They drive how we operate at the core. They are our belief system, our worldview. Private companies and nonprofits will often list their core values on their website. The idea of core values is widely embraced by many of the major religions of the world.

2. The next root issue is *behavior*. The main distinction between core values and behavior is core values dictate *what we believe* and behavior dictates *how we act*. Often our behavior will be a reflection of our core values or beliefs. Just like subsoil can be broken down into smaller layers, the same can be done with behavior. Behavior starts as a thought. The thought grows into action. The action grows into a habit. A habit grows into a behavior. A behavior grows into a culture. Behavior has different applications to different segments of society. Stephen Covey focused on habits in the business world when

writing the bestselling book called *The 7 Habits of Highly Effective People*. Psychology tells us that if we repeat something for twenty-one days, it becomes a habit. There is a science behind this category of behavior and, I believe, of root issues in general.

3. The next root issue is *natural ability*. This is the most visible root issue. It is easier to guess after a short period of time if someone has natural abilities in areas like sports, arts, business, or academics. It seems much easier to have a discussion around the root issue of natural abilities. Gallup has created a science from this root issue. Since the 1990s, they have identified thirty-plus specific strengths that humans may have. By buying a book such as *Strengths Finder 2*, written by Tom Rath, you will be invited to go online and go through a series of questions to determine your own personal top five strengths.

Root Dynamics

Bedrocks seem to only have one rule. If it remains a solid rock, we can build on it, and everything moves forward just fine. If it becomes broken or fractured, destruction can occur. Certainly we do not have to look very far to see the damage of earthquakes and the resulting tsunamis in our world that started with fractured bedrock. It is the same with core values. If they remain solid then everything moves forward just fine. If the core values become broken or fractured, destruction can occur. We only have to mention the broken core values of Adolf Hitler to see the amount of resulting destruction. History records Hitler as being responsible for the deaths of over 6 million Jews.[2]

Since bedrock is not visible from the surface, we tend to forget that it even exists. The same is true for core values. In the same way, it is easy to forget that core values even exist. After a while we may question if core values are even necessary, that is, until we see the destruction when core values are absent or forgotten.

What about altering the root issues? This is another dynamic to consider. If any one of the root categories is altered, it will impact the surface issues. Bedrock can be broken, subsoils can be polluted, and top soil can be eroded. All three need to remain in their original condition. All three need to stay in harmony with each other. Changing any one of the three can affect the garden above the surface. The same is true in the social and political realm.

For example, our core values in this nation as articulated in the Declaration of Independence were sound. It clearly states that all men are created equal. Yet our behaviors may be in conflict with our core values. By not dealing with the behavior of slavery, the result was the eventual destruction of over 600,000 lives during the Civil War, including a president. More deaths occurred during the Civil War than all American deaths from wars total since the Civil War. It is also important for natural abilities to not be altered and remain in harmony with the other root issues. If a business owner has great natural ability and uses their business savvy to start a Ponzi scheme, the natural ability is inconsistent with proper core values, and destruction occurs.

ARE YOU READY TO DIAGNOSE?

Let's continue to use the garden for diagnosing issues; this time, relate it back to solving problems in the social and political pyramid. The simplest problem is a pure surface issue with no root issue at all. A garden example is a potted plant that is not getting enough sun. Simply moving the plant to a better location fixes the problem. A surface solution is applied to a surface issue. No action is needed in the root area.

In actual problem solving, an example could be an elderly person who is too cold. Simply assisting the elderly person to a warmer location will solve the problem. A surface solution is applied to a surface issue. What starts to complicate the diagnosis is when we have a problem caused by different issues. The problem may be caused by both surface and root issues and this time needing two solutions, both a surface solution and a root solution.

If we have the same elderly person who is too cold, we may find that the root issue is poor circulation of their bloodstream to their extremities. The previous surface solution may satisfy the need in the short run, and a root solution will be needed for the long run. In this situation, we need both a surface solution and a root solution. The elderly person may need to be moved to a warmer location and at the same time have access to more exercise on a regular basis to generate more blood flow.

If we transition our problem solving to a national scale, we find many social issues have gotten more complex with more problems occurring at both the surface and root levels. Here is where the problem comes into play. The political structure responds with quick-fix surface solutions. The political structure does not seem to possess the needed ability to respond to the complexity of the social issues. The political structure dwells above the surface. Do you remember the first characteristic of the garden pyramid? Appreciating the value of both surface and root issues will determine the success of the gardener. If we want this nation to be successful, we need to get below the surface.

WHAT CAN YOU EXPECT?

So, here is what we are going to do in this book. We have selected three problems in America that are seemingly unrelated surface issues. The three issues are obesity, crime, and the national debt. We have selected these national issues because all three have roughly doubled within the last twenty-five years. In the garden, if three different vegetables are all wilting on the vine simultaneously, it is time to start looking at the root issues, too.

Before we move into chapter three, I want to show you one more important dynamic of root issues. It is the dynamic or root order. This will be the deepest we have dug so far into the root issues. We will begin to move away from the hypothetical and into real-life situations. I will not only start adding more substance to this subject, but I will also inject a lot of stories into the remainder of this chapter.

So, how important is it to keep the three root layers in order? Let's start with the garden pyramid. Remember the questions posed in the third characteristic root order? What would happen if we switched bedrock and subsoils around? Would it be a good place to build? We can also observe the same dynamic with the social and political pyramid. Keeping all three in the right order is important. What happens if core values and behaviors get reversed? Behavior is at the base, and core values are no longer the base. Have you seen examples of this in our society?

One could argue that in our nation's history, core values generally drove behavior. Today it would seem there are more examples of behavior driving core values. When I was a young adult, I was guilty of this myself. I would disregard core values and allow my behavior to be free. Hopefully I am improving in this area. However, if society over the long-run experiences behavior-driven core values, eventually the true core value goes away. It is a thing of the past. This can be true individually or as a society. If this were to happen to enough core values, we would move in the direction of a foundationless society. Depending on your philosophy in life, we would either be free or vulnerable. In this book, I would argue that a foundationless society would create vulnerability. I would personally promote a strong and positive root system built on strong and positive core values.

At the risk of sounding judgmental, let me identify a couple of specific examples of what happens when we change the order or hierarchy. What happens when we reverse core values and behavior? The first example is in politics and, specifically, negative campaign advertising. Somewhere along the line, a candidate had a devious thought. That devious thought turned into an action, and that candidate decided to run a smear campaign on a second candidate, resulting in the political destruction of that second candidate. This action did not stop there. The devious thought was now ready to graduate all the way up to a habit.

In 2006, I saw this approach being taught at a campaign school. It was not being discouraged; it was being encouraged as something to consider if the *opportunity* arises. Fast-forward to the month before the 2010 election. It was common to see twelve negative campaign ads during one thirty-minute television program. Guess what? The devious thought has now graduated into a full behavior within our society. Apparently most federal campaigns see an opportunity in every election.

The act of using negative campaign advertising began as a thought, progressed to an action, and grew into a habit. It has now become a behavior in the federal campaigns and will eventually become part of our culture. In the mind of the political leader, it is no longer seen as bad. And there it is; a behavior now drives the core value. Instead of showing respect for others as a core value in the political arena, multimillion-dollar budgets are used to destroy the reputation and image of others. MSNBC did a study in 2006 that showed even back then, 160 million dollars was spent on negative advertising in the U.S. Congressional races.[3]

My opinion is that a negative campaign may win in the short run, but it denigrates democracy in the long run. People are disgusted with the process and choose not to participate. They will still vote but will choose to stay away from grassroots politics or running for political office themselves.

Let me share a personal experience that will demonstrate the degree of premeditation and investment into damaging an opponent's image.

It was a cold Minnesota morning with snow blowing across Interstate 90. The snow wasn't so bad; it was the ice and glaze coating the blacktop that made us nervous. As we traveled across bridges heading west, our car would gradually slide from side to side. My policy director was driving as we headed to Worthington High School. The school had a long-time agreement with the city to provide local cable news to the community. We were scheduled to be there at 10 a.m. to do an on-air recording in regard to my campaign and specific to the national debt.

As we prepared to start filming, we noticed that someone else who had been hanging around the studio pulled out a video camera and started recording as well. We asked the station camera operator about the additional camera. He shared with us that since the facility is inside a public school, it is owned by the public. Therefore, it is open to the public for anyone to attend these events. The public property part made sense, but the question that stuck in our head was this: What was so vitally important that someone would dare to be on these roads? Someone who was not even obligated to be here? The weather conditions were absolutely treacherous. Someone would be risking their life to be traveling from anywhere outside the city of Worthington just to videotape this event.

After some gentle probing, the gentleman in question admitted he was on staff with a major political party for the purpose of tracking our activities. He said he personally did not feel it was right to lie about it, so he admitted it. Hmm. So, what do we have here? In plain terms, he could be considered a political stalker. He was not stalking to hurt us physically. He was there in preparation to damage our image and reputation. I had never given much thought to the degree of premeditation to negative advertising. I just assumed that an accidental piece of video ended up in the wrong hands, and it was used to damage opponents in a political race. I never thought about the idea that political leaders would need to deliberately plan a stalking strategy years before an election, set up a budget that would allow enough staffing and equipment to execute the stalking, and have this endeavor up and running ten months before the election. The staff, after being hired, would need to be committed to the point of pushing through treacherous conditions to complete their mission. Now I know politics is very competitive, but this is something that, when experienced firsthand, speaks volumes to the character of what we are dealing with.

As the year went on, we experienced the same gentleman again as well as variations of this type of action coming in and out of our camp and allegedly even into the organizational meetings within our campaign.

As we left Worthington, MN, that cold winter day, I thought to myself, *Wow! I hope I never become that desperate to directly associate myself with stalkers.*

I do not blame anyone personally for this character flaw in our political culture; I am not going to talk about which party this situation was representing, because that is not the purpose of the story. The purpose of the story is to demonstrate what happens when behaviors drive core values rather than core values driving behaviors.

It does not stop there. Today there is collateral damage. Major corporations in the private sector are targeting their competition with negative advertising. This behavior progresses one last time into a cultural issue. It is no longer isolated to one sector.

Another example of behaviors driving core values also comes from the political sector. My wife, Jeanne, and I were watching a cable news channel in 2005. We were experiencing a popular evening program for the first time. After just a few minutes, I said to my wife, "Why are they yelling? We can hear them just fine without the yelling." She agreed. What we experienced next was one commentator cutting the other commentator off during their comments. This really bothered my wife and still does today. Because of this behavior over the last few years, people now *expect* this type of discourteous discourse in the media. As a matter of fact, it has now become entertainment. We have combined the mood of the World Wrestling Federation interviews with our nation's current events. The point is that our new behaviors are driving core values. Instead of having the self-discipline of letting someone else finish before speaking, we now seem to get points for on-air bullying. Once again, behaviors are driving core values rather than core values driving our behaviors.

I will give you a personal experience with this root issue as well. I had the opportunity to participate in all shapes and sizes of debates and forums during a run for U.S. Congress. From a large metro debate in Minneapolis to small classrooms in rural Minnesota, I became savvier on debate dynamics and better at cutting my opponents off in mid-sentence, striking back with a verbal response before the opponent could finish their sentence. I was now adapting to the behavior and doing so in a negative manner. As a matter of fact, I was starting to embrace the behavior.

I was unsuccessful in the race, and a few months after the election, I interviewed for a job with a major U.S. corporation. A few days after the interview, the company recruiter gave me some feedback on my performance in the interview. His first comment was that I cut off the interviewer twice during our discussion. His follow-up comment was that the act of cutting others off demonstrates the inability to be teachable. Now to be fair, there were some other things in play. But it does demonstrate the downside to allowing the political culture to spill over into mainstream behavior. In other words, I was becoming a jerk. My behaviors were starting to affect my core values and eat away at my respect for other people.

I have just shared with you some examples of behavior-driven core values in politics. I will also provide an example of this dynamic within the social arena in chapter four.

The garden has much to teach us about the unseen things in life. The conditions above the ground can be an indicator of the conditions below the ground. In the same way, I hope the problem-solving pyramid can help us diagnose problems less visible under the surface.

The last thing we will do in this chapter is use the social and political pyramid to help us understand one of the most significant mistakes made in our nation today. I call it "Pruning the Problem." You will want to read this short vignette.

PRUNING THE PROBLEM

Do you remember back in chapter one when we talked about the different way we approach good plants versus bad weeds? With good plants, we prune back the plant to get even more plant. With bad weeds, we need to go below the surface and pull out the root. But what happens when we prune the bad weed? As a result, we would see most of the problem go away. We know from experience the weed comes back and many times with even more determination than before. If we continue to use the same strategy of managing weeds, we will soon be dealing with a bigger weed, and it will require more action, bigger equipment, more money, and more time. A continuation of this strategy would seem ridiculous. Eventually the weeds take over the garden.

Many times in the social and political arena, we embrace this same strategy of "pruning the problem." We have an obvious surface issue, and we pass a political remedy that satisfies the problem in the short run, and we all feel better. A few years later, a political or government leader will point to the issue and argue that we did not allocate enough money and soon attack the surface issue with more of the same action, bigger programs, more money, and more time. Then it happens again a few years later. I will give a specific example in chapter seven.

In our nation, I would argue this strategy has been one of the flaws of handling government social programs. This "pruning the problem" has contributed to the cost of entitlement programs. Today we are at a tipping point. Entitlement programs are consuming roughly 50 percent of our nation's budget and will take over the social and political garden if we ignore the root issues. I realize the aging population is the surface issue, but we also have root issues that I believe are just as significant.

The garden simply needs gardeners willing to pull out the weeds by the roots. The nation simply needs leaders who can be courageous and identify solutions that allow root issues to be addressed. In this book, the solutions will come in chapter nine.

In the next three chapters, we clearly identify surface issues affecting our nation that can be traced back to root issues. We will use these three chapters as case studies that will clearly support our method and approach to root issues. We begin in chapter three with case study #1 and the issue of obesity.

ROOT LESSON FROM CHAPTER TWO:

What is unseen can affect our life as
much as what is seen.

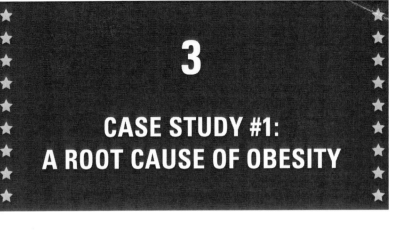

3

CASE STUDY #1:
A ROOT CAUSE OF OBESITY

When you were in grade school, did you have that kid in your class that you just did not know what to do with? What made it worse is they never moved away. The popular kids moved away but not this one. Perhaps they were overweight, smelled funny, or wore glasses at an early age. As you moved into junior high, you wondered, *What good will ever come from this kid?*

Well, guess what? I was that kid. As I moved through grade school, I was that overweight, smelly, crossed-eyed kid who wore glasses. And I would have to admit, I could relate to my peers who asked, "What will ever come of this kid?"

I am mixing a little humor and truth together right now. What I am saying is this: I was overweight in grade school and spent most of my adult life overweight. Therefore, I can relate to this subject. I know it can be hard for minorities to climb the corporate or political ladder. But how many overweight, cross-eyed people do you see in leadership? The cross-eyed part is out of one's control. And yet for many (not all), our weight can be reduced. So, why does the number of obese people in the U.S. continue to skyrocket? As a matter of fact, obesity has doubled in the last twenty-five years.

Figure 2. Trends in overweight, obesity and extreme obesity, ages 20-73 years

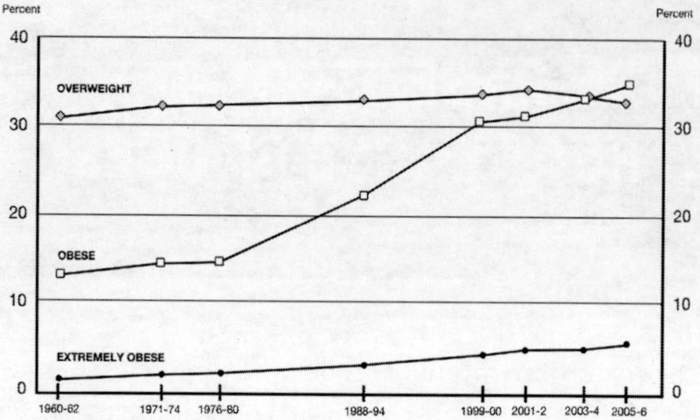

Note: Age-adjusted by the direct method to the year 2000 US Bureau of the Census using age groups 20-39, 40-59 and 60-74 years. Pregnant females excluded. Overweight defined as 25<=BMI<30; obesity defines as BMI>=30; Extreme obesity defines as BMI>=40.

What is that about? What is the root issue? Obesity is a surface issue. I want to know a root issue!

For nearly a decade, I worked with at-risk youth and their families. In the year 2000, I started a nonprofit that is now called Bridge Builders for Kids. The non-profit worked mainly with children who have a parent in prison. More and more we work with the parents as well. When I was working with the nonprofit as the executive director, we had retreat-style conferences for the entire family who were outside of prison.

One day we were driving the bus from the ranch to the conference center. It was a short drive of maybe twenty-five minutes. Since many of these families are in poverty, we absolutely made sure we went above and beyond in providing nutritious food and plenty of it. We had just provided snacks before getting on the bus, and we would be serving supper shortly after arriving back at the conference center. Then something happened that caught my attention. Despite the short trip, someone asked to stop and use a restroom. No big deal, we pulled into a convenience store and parked to let the individual off the bus. What happened next is what caught me off guard. Many of the people got off the bus and returned with family-sized bags of chips and twelve-packs of pop. As individuals, they dove into the family-sized portions immediately.

At first I was a little offended because I was proud of the attention we had given to providing for their nutritional and individual needs. The more I have pondered this situation, the more I have realized it was not a slam against our meals and quantity of food. There was something else going on. Even after all the food they had received, their hand was essentially still on the refrigerator door. I would have to admit, there may have been a type of judgment going on in my own mind at this point. However, as time passed, I have looked at my own life and realized that oftentimes I get up from the table stuffed to the gills and find my hand on the refrigerator door a few minutes later.

This story tells me there must be a root issue down there someplace. For me, I could try a new diet every Tuesday and my weight would not change because I am not dealing with the root issue. The weight problem is the surface issue. I am not saying this is the case for everyone, but for many of us, there is a root issue underneath the surface issue of obesity. I personally believe understanding the root issue will help us to understand the surging increases of obesity in this nation today.

In case you have not heard of the idea before, let me introduce you to something called emotional eating. In this chapter, we will not only explore emotional eating but look for a root issue that drives its engine, and then look at some possible solutions.

Before we move into emotional eating, we will look at two references on the subject. The first is a study I will reference again later in this book. It is a comprehensive study called the ACE Study. The Adverse Childhood Experiences (ACE) Study[5] is one of the largest investigations ever conducted to assess associations between childhood maltreatment and later-life health and well-being. The study is a collaboration between the Centers for Disease Control and Prevention and Kaiser Permanente's Health Appraisal Clinic in San Diego. The ACE Study findings suggest that certain *childhood* experiences are major risk factors for the leading causes of *adult* illness and death in the United States. These childhood experiences are also major risk factors for a poor quality of life. This study demonstrates the link between childhood experiences and adult behavior. As we dig into this study, we find one of the health risk behaviors is obesity.

A conclusion of this specific part of the ACE study is contained in this statement: "Abuse in childhood is associated with adult obesity. If causal, preventing child abuse may modestly decrease adult obesity. Treatment of obese adults abused as children may benefit from identification of mechanisms that lead to maintenance of adult obesity."[6]

Two ideas were brought to light in this quote. First, a root cause is identified, and that is child abuse. This is the first specific root issue I am identifying in this book. As a matter of fact, in the next two chapters, we will discuss trauma in young children in more depth. Obesity is the surface issue, and child abuse is the root issue. The second idea from the ACE study is that treating adults is beneficial. There are likely millions of people in America who are emotionally eating and have not taken the time to think about why they are emotionally eating. That will be the focus of this chapter.

Before we move on, I want to give you just a bit more detail from this study that you will find helpful. The individual study specific to obesity explained that the two childhood abuses most strongly associated with body weight and obesity were physical and verbal abuse. If we look at the number of reported physical abuses and emotional abuses from the study, it was 28.3 percent and 10.6 percent respectively of the more than 17,000 surveyed.[7] What does this mean for our discussion? It means that emotional eating could have the potential of impacting tens of millions of Americans. It means people should spend a little less time dealing with the latest dieting fad and spend a little more time asking questions about their childhood. It means as individuals, we should consider possible root issues first.

A second reference is from the Mayo Clinic. Since I am from Minnesota, I need to reference the Mayo Clinic early in the book! They have issued a paper on the concept of emotional eating as well. The article was written by Mayo Clinic staff in 2009 and can be found on their website. The article not only points to life events as a trigger to emotional eating but also the hassles of current everyday life. This would indicate that both stress of the past and stress of today are triggers for emotional eating. What about that hand on the refrigerator door? The report had this to say: "In fact, your emotions may become so tied to your eating habits that you automatically reach for a sweet treat whenever you're angry or stressed without stopping to think about what you're doing."[8]

There is one key element of emotional eating that you should look for in this chapter that I believe is a key driver causing this root issue to become so strong. Grab a nice bag of carrots, and let's get started. During the course of this book, I will introduce you to three Minnesota friends who will articulate root issues much better than I could. My first Minnesota friend is Don Carlson. Don comes from a brilliant family of thinkers. Their family alone could establish a think tank and do very well for themselves. Of anyone I have talked to about this issue, I believe Don can do the best job of introducing and explaining emotional eating and how you and I can begin to deal with this in our own individual lives. I will join you again at the end of the chapter. Here's Don:

> Gosh, it's depressing to watch the news if you're overweight. Even if you're not, it's hard to see the parade of stories showing up about the number of Americans who are overweight, childhood obesity, future costs to Medicare caused by obesity, research looking at the

dangers of trans fat, high-fructose corn syrup, salt, cholesterol, and so on. After the opening news stories, the commercial break promotes the latest junk food to come down the pike, steaming hot, with twice as many calories as a pro-football lineman would need in a day. After the break, we get the stories about how stress levels in this country are going through the roof, teenage pregnancies are high, divorce rates are troublesome, school achievement ratings lag behind other countries, and how all of the job losses are continuing. Then, it's time for the next commercial. This time we get to hear about the latest antidepressant, which has no sexual side effects. All these messages persist about how unhappy we are and how our quality of life is decreasing. Maybe the first step is to turn off the television. But we all know that won't fix anything by itself.

For those of us who have struggled with a weight problem, we have a sense that there is a very profound connection between our emotional *self* and our *weight*. You have heard the question: which came first, the chicken or the egg? For us, the question is: which came first, being overweight or fostering a troublesome and painful relationship with food that comes with being overweight?

Taking a step back, it would be helpful to bring some insight into this mystery. We all have events in our lives that have had a role in shaping our character. We can name many of them: births, deaths, tragic accidents, abuse, romance, divorce, and others quickly come to mind. But a huge portion of who we are is as much formed by millions of smaller choices and experiences. Think of it like a mosaic: a group of innumerable pieces of color, all put together to form a portrait of who we are. Throughout Europe there are many pieces of art that were done with mosaic. Artisans carefully selected from thousands of different colors of glass or ceramics to create works of art that would stand the test of time. Many are fabulously ornate. The journey to finding weight loss and happiness will be similar. It probably will not be one big, life-changing event. Rather think of it as a venture where the bits of color are being removed, one by one. New colors are put in place, so that over time the portrait changes and evolves. Bit by bit, you will find a new you: a happier, healthier you.

Several years ago, I ran into my friend George (not his real name), as he had completed a diet a few months before. He had successfully plummeted from over 300 pounds to somewhere in the neighborhood of 180 pounds. He had used the low-carbohydrate diet that was very popular at the time. While he was very pleased with the new closet full of clothes he was forced to buy, he was already seeing the first signs of his weight heading back upward. He commented, "If you ever meet anyone in this world who wants to *gain* weight, the first thing you need to tell them is, 'Go on a *diet*.' It works every time." In all the years since I first met George, this has been his story. He has lived the weight-loss rollercoaster with the most dramatic weight swings that I have ever seen. Last time I crossed paths with George, his weight was higher than at any time I had ever known him.

Why is it that dieting and weight loss turn out this way for so many people? Let me give you a brief example, and see if you can identify with this situation. Let's imagine a middle-aged man named Joe. (Joe is the composite of a number of people I've known, including myself!) He's generally healthy, with a good metabolism. Joe knows that he's carrying more weight than is good for him. He is sixty pounds overweight. While he hasn't dieted lately, he remembers that dieting is a real headache. Depriving himself of food when hunger strikes has always been a nightmare. The frustration he feels when all of the weight comes right back has been doubly aggravating. Even though he doesn't like the extra weight, Joe currently finds that if he keeps his food intake at about 3,500 calories on average, he can keep his 250-pound weight pretty stable. Hence, we can say that the general metabolic functioning of his body plus the energy he burns in his daily activity equals 3,500 calories.

One day Joe musters all of the enthusiasm and motivation he can, and begins a new weight-loss diet. He does his homework and chooses a reasonably well-balanced, 1,500-calorie-per-day diet, which will allow him to lose weight fairly quickly, and he hopes that it won't leave him totally miserable. Joe has heard that it's not a great idea to lose weight too quickly.

So, Joe starts reading labels, evaluating what he eats, measuring and weighing. As the first days go by, he realizes that he's usually a little low on energy, often hungry, and almost constantly thinking of food. What made it all worthwhile was having the bathroom scale work its way downward. That was fun to watch. Two months of the struggle, and Joe has had enough. He steps on the scale and sees that he has lost twenty pounds … yippee! The clothes are fitting better. The mirror is looking good. It's fun to be able to bounce out of a chair and go for a walk. Joe tells himself that it's a good time to take a break from dieting for a little while. His intentions are good. In a few weeks, he wants to do this again, hoping to drop another twenty pounds.

But evil lurks in the shadows. As Joe is out enjoying his trimmer physique, he doesn't quite realize that his body has changed some over the course of the past two months. Joe's body was not as thrilled with his diet. While Joe jumped into those first days of the diet, his body got the message that a famine was beginning, and it was time to switch into *starvation mode*. It responded in two ways. First, it started turning down the metabolic thermostat, so Joe's body wouldn't use so much energy in his day-to-day activities. Secondly, Joe stepped on the scale and saw that he had lost twenty pounds, but what he didn't realize was that some of the weight he had lost was due to his lower salt intake over the course of the diet. Hence, what Joe really lost was sixteen pounds of fat and four pounds of water. (Had Joe been on a really severe diet, he might have also lost some amount of muscle mass. This would have further undermined his ability to maintain a lower weight in that the energy burning *muscle engine* would have become smaller. During starvation, the body can survive with less muscle, but once the fat is gone, you are done.)

Several days after Joe began what he considers a maintenance diet, he steps on the scale and is shocked to see that he has bounced up five pounds. Joe suffered a sort of dietary *whiplash*. His body had not yet come out of *starvation mode*. When it saw that there were a few extra calories floating around that hadn't been there for a while, it packed away every calorie it could back into the fat cells so that it could survive the famine. To add insult to injury, Joe had gotten a bit more relaxed about his salt intake, so his water weight went right back up.

Joe was heartbroken. This was going to be just like all the other diets he'd tried over the years. He knew in his head that to stay on the maintenance diet, he had to stay disciplined, but he was so tired of all the weighing and measuring. He could do without all of that. A couple weeks later, Joe stepped on the scale and saw two more pounds had returned. He was ashamed of himself. Why did he have such a terrible lack of self-control? That evening he had a decent supper, but before he went to bed, he found himself frustrated. He looked up to see his hand on the refrigerator door.

"Why am I doing this?" he asked himself. "I'm really not hungry."

But the door opened, and inside was a leftover piece of cheesecake that his wife brought home from a party. It had been sitting there for a couple days and would go bad if somebody didn't eat it.

After a couple more weeks of this, Joe grew angrier with himself and decided it was time to rally. A few days of weighing and measuring went okay, but he knew his heart wasn't in it. After a while, he slid back to the maintenance diet for a few weeks. He tried leveling off for a month or two, but it was depressing to step on the bathroom scale. More and more often, he found that the late-night sandwich and the extra helping of pasta seemed to soothe some of the pain and loneliness as his clothes were getting tight again. The least painful course was to simply stop stepping on the scale.

Joe started feeling guilty and ashamed that he had ever tried such a foolish thing in the first place. His wife and all of the folks who had been supportive as he was losing weight were now seemingly showing him pity. Trying to control his eating habits was like trying to swim upstream: a lot of work and no evidence of progress. In fact, he was going backward. You can guess how this story ends. It ends the same way for Joe as it has for most of us. In the end, Joe had a few new pounds to carry around, together with a fresh bundle of painful, unhealthy emotions.

You perhaps have heard the definition of insanity: trying the same thing over and over again and continuing to expect different results. To compound this insanity comes a thousand weight-loss plans, each encouraging you to use the same basic strategy with some new twist. The cover of every weight-loss book or magazine has a photograph of what you should look like after you have completed the diet, encouraging you to seek the new, slender, sexy you.

An important step in understanding how things can work differently for you is to first grasp a key concept: it's not about the food. It's about your *relationship* with the food. This is the driver Steven mentioned earlier in the chapter.

For most of us, the first relational bond that we formed came from receiving food from a loving mother. As we grew, food became a powerful symbol for how our parents cared and provided for us. Mealtimes were often occasions for us to gather together and share in the connectedness that families can enjoy. We may have picked up bits and pieces from the media and surrounding culture that enjoying the right food or beverage would make you attractive or popular. Food became a method by which you could control your life. How many children get through their early years without some power struggles with their parents over what they will or won't eat? You figure out that if you eat something with sugar, it tastes good, and it will also give you an energy boost. You learn that if you overeat, it will make you more relaxed, even tired. It seems to relieve stress and help you relax and fall asleep. You have heard the phrase *comfort food*. It's strange how often that expression is used. Perhaps it provides a good reminder to you how closely tied food is to your feeling of well-being.

While some of these phenomena are bio-chemical facts, others are mixed with emo-tional and psychological meanings that we have attached to food. As you look at how you have come to relate to food, you begin to see that it can become a way by which you find comfort, relief from stress, a response to shame or guilt, a way to resolve grief or anger, and even a way to deal with depression. In other words, you have spent a lot of years developing a relationship with the food. Think about it. It is almost as though food has become a significant person in your life whom you can go to for the purpose of having your emotional needs met. If you go to food for comfort, intimacy, relief from stress or depression, etc., food may have become one of your closest companions.

If this is a topic you have interest in learning more about, Don has provided more personal insights in the back of this book.

You have just finished reading some great insights on emotional eating from one of my guest contribu-tors, Don Carlson. Don has helped me personally. I lost thirty pounds the year I was in Iraq, and Don has been helping me keep that weight off. It can be a struggle for me every day. I am one of those who can find my hand on the refrigerator door far too often. My daughter, Brittany, said the other day, "Dad just finished his third breakfast." She is in college studying psychology. Anytime she comes home, she is reminded of the demand for her profession. So lately, I have been pondering the question, "What do I really need?"

Over the course of several weeks, I have come up with two answers to my reasons for overeating. Both of them are personal. The first is this: I am finding that over the years, my wife and I have lost our knack for finding fun activities. We went out to eat with two dear friends, Todd and Dianne, the other night, and Todd reminded me that I was the guy always having fun in college. Now, my kids are grown, and I am writing a book while my wife goes to work every day. How boring is that? I need to become who I really am again. Food is not the right answer. There are healthier alternatives.

My second reason for overeating is the more personal of the two. When I was growing up, I had a bit of a dysfunctional father. He died when I was ten. Because of my father's dysfunction in parenting, I came away from my youth with a low self-image. As I grew into adulthood, I found that I was susceptible to rejection. I have dealt with these issues of self-image and rejection with a lot of help from others, including my family. My core values are now on a healthier track. However, there is still some residual behavior even though the root problem is gone. By using a core value of forgiveness, the problem can be gone, but I am behaving like the problem is still there. With Don's help, I am gradually changing my habits by asking myself, "What do

I really need?" and then thinking through a fun list of alternatives.

The next chapter will deal with a root issue of crime. Remember, things like crime are a surface issue. We will find a lot to talk about when we get under the surface. It will likely affect you personally more than you could anticipate.

ROOT LESSON FROM CHAPTER THREE:

We are all wired to have relationships; we just need to choose the right ones.

4

CASE STUDY #2:
A ROOT CAUSE OF CRIME

THE CAMP

He was the last one to join our group. We had been waiting for some time now, and the rest of the people were getting impatient. Patience is difficult for any child, and it was especially true for these children as these kids either had a mom or a dad in prison. Today was supposed to be different. Today was supposed to be more relaxed and free of the anxieties of life. Today we were on our way to summer camp.

As the camp director, it was my responsibility to make sure everyone was safe. Bobby had been dropped off along with his two sisters by their uncle, and now Bobby had gone inside the church for some unknown reason. I could not find him in the entrance area, so as I began to walk inside the boys' bathroom, I immediately saw Bobby with blood smeared over his hands and arms. Upon my arrival into the bathroom, he quickly cleaned himself up, and we walked toward the waiting bus.

This was the first time I had met Bobby, and he kept a safe distance from me. It was obvious this eleven-year-old boy had been cutting himself and, like the rest of the kids on that bus, struggling on the inside to make sense of his life. For them, it was hard to communicate their struggle with the rest of the world. These kids had been in survival mode for so long, they did not know anything else.

From that point through the second day of camp, Bobby looked for attention and acceptance by his peers. His method of communicating the problems on the inside was to be disruptive on the outside. He was disruptive in almost every event that occurred in every situation. Like many camps before, I tried to work with the most challenging kids. After two days, I had tried almost everything I could think of to moderate Bobby's constant loud distractions from the activities at hand.

Finally, as we were sitting in a camp meeting with the other youth, I looked over at Bobby sitting next to me. Having hit the bottom of the list of ideas, I said, "Bobby, do you want to go outside and play Frisbee?"

For the first time in those two days, he stopped what he was doing and looked right at me. After a few seconds, in a calm voice, he said, "Just you and me?"

Taken back by the fact that this was the first time he engaged in a short but real conversation, I said, "Sure, Bobby, just you and me."

Obviously, at that point we slipped out the back of the room and went outside to spend some time together. Then something very simple happened. One child was having one-to-one time with one adult in a nurturing and safe environment. As I was playing Frisbee with Bobby, part of my attention was on Bobby and part of my brain was processing what Bobby had just communicated. This whole idea of one-to-one positive adult nurturing seemed so simple, yet it was obviously something that was not that simple or available to these kids. Perhaps Bobby had just found a way to communicate to the rest of the world what he needed without even realizing it. The environment he was responding to was a safe environment that only included a caring adult, no other competition from his peers, and lastly an environment that was free from trauma. No one was going to hurt him emotionally or otherwise.

As child after child and camp after camp and year after year went by, I continued to process the idea of time and trauma with children. As a camp, we made changes to reflect the needs of our kids. Eventually, we moved to one counselor for every camper. We also decreased the size of the camps to decrease the perceived subtle trauma of peer pressure. Changing the time and trauma elements of the camps completely changed the tension in the air. Working with twenty to thirty at-risk youths at a time in a residential setting can be a bit stressful. After making the needed adjustments, the camps became much more enjoyable for the kids and the adult volunteers.

I have spent a decade working with at-risk youth and their families, and I still perk up my ears when I hear a child tell us what is really happening on the inside. More recently, for example, I was helping at a camp for children of prisoners just for a day. As I was walking on a hiking trail in the woods with some kids and adults, one of the boys was walking behind me. All of a sudden, he launched his body through the air and landed on my back for a piggyback ride. Even though it surprised me to now be carrying a 120-pound boy on my back, I heard him say after a few minutes, "Now I am going to have some special time too, just like other kids."

I have come to believe these quiet messages from our children are profound. The more I look at this issue, the more I am convinced it is the biggest social issue of our day. As an American society, we are not spending enough time with our children in the home. As we go through the chapters in this book, I hope to show you that this issue is likely costing our nation 1 to 5 percent of the economy. In other words, hundreds of billions of dollars are being spent *reactively*, instead of hundreds of billions being spent *proactively* in some other manner by our society.

This social flaw has been growing for about one hundred years, mostly the last forty years. Very little attention seems to be given to this major issue. During the 2008 presidential campaign season and in the 2010 election, very little was even mentioned about it. It is not something that gets votes. What did get the attention of voters in 2008? The cost of health care. So, what is the difference? Health care is moving large chunks of dollars out of the pockets of most Americans. However, the cost of not spending time with our children gets fiscally spread out across many areas of our society. The cost shows up in the criminal justice system, our education system, our welfare system, and in the nonprofit sector. Too many young men and women are preparing for prison and pregnancy rather than for their first job or marriage.

We also need to consider the reduced revenue that occurs as these at-risk youth enter adulthood. State and federal tax revenue is not realized, FICA payments are not realized, and real estate taxes are not realized.

In order to help bring this important issue to light, I will show you a tool in this chapter that can predict the probability of a specific eight-year-old child going to prison, graduating from high school, and even owning a home someday. It is based on a theoretical concept of time and trauma, and I think you will be intrigued.

This is the second root issue I will demonstrate in this book. Crime is the surface issue. The lack of enough quantity and quality time we spend with our children is a root issue of crime. It is a simple concept, but the impact on our society is far from simple. I believe the impact is complex and dramatic. I think you will find it quite compelling.

TIME

So, what do scientists say about the lack of time spent with our children? Let's look at what the American Psychological Association said about the issue of time with our nation's youth. In a June/July 2003 issue of the *American Psychologist*, a study was discussed that said this: "Youth problems are unacceptably high … parents are spending less time parenting…. 240 hours per year."[9] This research occurred between 1989 and 2003. The study clearly links parenting time with success or, in this case, the lack of parenting time with a lack of success.

Let's take a look at the history of time associated with nurturing children. During the preindustrial revolution, Ma and Pa were generally in the home and involved in farming or other family business. What did that mean in terms of time around their children? The amount of time children experienced with a nurturing adult in the home could have easily been three, four, or five hours per day. Average hours per year could have been between one thousand and two thousand hours. Keep in mind grandparents were often living in the home as well. It is feasible that yearly hours of nurturing could have been over two thousand per year.

When the industrial revolution began, dads started spending less time at home; however, nurturing hours could have still been well over a thousand.

During the mid-1900s, grandparents started living outside the home of their children. Although it meant more independence for the grandparents and less responsibility to care for the elderly from the adult children, there have been losers in these situations. Grandchildren gradually received fewer hours of nurturing in the home.

In the 1960s and 1970s, both parents started working away from home. These last two changes likely reduced time with children to a thousand or even five hundred hours of nurturing per child per year.

Beginning in the 1960s, fathers started abandoning their families, forcing mothers to take on the full responsibility of the home. Single mothers found themselves with one or two jobs outside the home, and these last two evolving changes left many children with fewer than 500 hours per year of nurturing in the home.

In the last hundred years as a whole, we may have seen a drop of a thousand hours of nurturing time per year for some children. A child growing up in 1912 may have had access to four adults in the house, and a child growing up in 2012 may have little access to any adults in his or her household.

The study in the *American Psychologist* article showed a 240-hour per year drop since 1989.[10] This information would be consistent with the history over the last one hundred years.

Meanwhile, back at the ranch (camp), we had yet to discover the information above, and were compelled to do some backyard research of our own. In 2003, our camp was partnering with another nonprofit called Parenting with Purpose. One of the staff members was a University of Minnesota student. She was working with children of prisoners as well. She agreed to do some loose-knit research to try out our theory of time with children. She compared twenty children in a control group of successful children in a neighborhood to twenty children of prisoners in the same neighborhood of the same demographics. The twenty children who were in the control group were doing well in school and were engaged in their community in some way outside of school. The children of prisoners were marginal in both school performance and community engagement.

So, the big question is, what was the difference in time and trauma that was being experienced in the home with these two groups of children? First, we had to develop a system of analyzing the situation in the home and quantifying the results. Some consideration was given to the trauma in the home, but most of the consideration was given to hours of time in the home. Then we came up with a name for the theory and arrived at "Positive-Adult Nurturing," or "PAN Time."

The results were this: the successful children in the control group were experiencing over 1,000 hours per year of positive-adult nurturing or PAN time in the home, and the less successful group of children was experiencing an average of 361 hours of PAN time. PAN time was given a value of one hour when it occurred with one adult and no other children. Two children with one adult was given a value of .5 hours and so on. The most PAN time a child could get in one hour was one hour, no matter how many adults were in the room.

Now I realize this data is from backyard research and the samples are small in number, but it gave us what we needed to put more confidence in this PAN-time theory and make changes in our organization that would serve our children better. Here are some of those resulting actions:

1. Another forty youth were assessed after the initial study at Parenting with Purpose. This continued to give us more confidence in the PAN-time theory. We could actually see the correlation between the behavior in the child and the calculated assessment number on paper. One time in particular, we were very surprised. We did the PAN-time assessment on a teenage boy

whom we considered to be relatively functional and low risk. However, the PAN-time number came up low for him, meaning high risk. Two years later, he was arrested at age sixteen. Anecdotal as it may be, our interest in the PAN-time theory grew.

2. Major changes were made to program areas, with the size of camp reduced to an average of five to ten kids at a time. The ratios of available adults to kids were almost always one to one. This provides more of a family atmosphere. It is also the opposite direction of almost every other camp. Most camps are working on economies of scale. Our camp felt the need to go the opposite direction with no economy of scale. If this type of ratio is really needed to be effective, what does this mean for our public school system as the population of at-risk youth continues to increase in our society? Is it possible that in our public schools today, we have students that are still seeing 1,000-plus hours of PAN time per year and other students with 300 hours of PAN time per year sitting next to them? And if this is true, does it mean something as we look at education? Does it give us any hint as to the source of the achievement gap in America, keeping in mind that *education starts in the home*?

3. It became obvious that the camp alone was not enough. To have even a minor effect on the lives of these children, a mentoring organization

would be needed. Therefore, a new organization was added in 2003 called Bridge Builders for Kids. Now the kids had their own camp in the summer and a caring, adult mentor year-round. The kids are now receiving at least 100 additional hours of PAN time per year from outside the home. It is a small part of what many of these youth need, but it's a start.

Later in this chapter, we will look at some specific categories and trends of time with children in the U.S. First, we will look at the issue of trauma and then time and trauma together.

TRAUMA

The most traumatic thing that can happen to a child is the voluntary abandonment of a parent. It is something we have all worried about when we were young. What will happen if I lose my mom or dad? Even harder for us to believe as a young person is the scenario of our mom or dad intentionally or voluntarily leaving us. Today, dads are often leaving their children thirty minutes after conception. If I am the product of a one-night stand, what does that do for my perception of family, commitment, and love? Does that affect my self-image? Most times, the trauma is brought on by the actions or inactions of the father. Trauma seems to happen more easily in a home with a dysfunctional father or a home without any father present. Either way, it often starts with the father and his role as a parent.

These trauma issues are not excluded from two-parent homes. I am going to walk you through a series of rhetorical questions to help you understand the emotional trauma that a child may experience. What happens if a child's dad is involved in his/her life but is a dysfunctional father? What happens if he constantly tells that child that he/she is worthless, and that he/she is only a liability to this earth? What does that do for that child's self-image? How many years will that self-image continue to stay with that child? How will this trauma manifest itself in the actions of this child throughout his/her adult years?

What happens if a dad ends up on the wrong side of the law? How much trauma is injected into a child who watches his/her dad or mom being arrested and physically removed from the home? And what happens if that child waits three years for his/her parent to return from prison and finally experiences joy with the return of the parent, only to see the parent re-arrested? Keep in mind re-arrests or recidivism rates have approached 60-plus percent in this nation.[11]

This time the parent is arrested for five years. This time the mother is getting tired and lonely and starts having boyfriends visit the home. What happens if these boyfriends start acting as pseudo parents and then vanish after six months? Now how much voluntary abandonment has this child experienced in his/her short lifetime? What happens if one of those pseudo parents physically or sexually abuses that child? Much attention is given to the actions of the adults, but what is the child experiencing?

Are all these questions even a reality? Do these situations really occur?

Let's take a look at one study conducted by an organization called All Children Excel located in St. Paul, Minnesota.[12] The Ramsey County group works with ten-year-old children who have committed a crime. Here are some of their findings from one group of children they worked with:

- 91 percent had a parent incarcerated

- 81 percent experienced intervention from a child protection agency

- 76 percent experienced parent drug use

- 63 percent experienced domestic violence

It should be noted that this was a very small number of children who reported experiencing this level of trauma. At this point, one could only speculate on the national trends. However, we do know the numbers of younger-aged criminals are growing rapidly. Even U.S. cities with populations around 100,000 are now experiencing ten-year-old offenders in reportable numbers. For example, Rochester, Minnesota, is the home of the world-famous Mayo Clinic. According to Morgan Quitno Press,[13] Rochester is one of America's safest metropolitan areas. Yet the city seemingly continues to wrestle with increased gang activity and crimes by younger adolescents.

So, what happens when a child is experiencing a high degree of trauma in his/her life? What are the results? Just a note before moving forward: you may find in this book that I refer to children of prisoners. Another term is children of incarcerated parents;

however, in most instances, these terms could easily be exchanged for at-risk youth.

Here is what the Child Welfare League had to say about trauma in youth as it relates to crime: "Some studies show posttraumatic stress disorder (PTSD) rates among youth in the justice system may be up to eight times as high as rates of other similar age peers."[14]

Wow! This starts to help us understand a little more about what causes some children to act the way they do. So what actually happens inside a child between the trauma and the violent act? The Child Welfare League goes on to say:

> Exposure to trauma … can have a number of deleterious and long-lasting effects on how teenagers see the world and the way they function socially, interpersonally, and academically. It can affect their behavior, their problem-solving skills, and their ability to modulate their emotions, and it can eventually give rise to patterns of conflict and aggression toward others.

I had to look up the word "deleterious" used in this quote. According to *Webster's Dictionary*, it means: "harmful often in a subtle or unexpected way."[15] Hmm. One of the unexpected ways I have personally experienced with at-risk kids is a delay in their emotional and mental development. I think this emotional and mental delay can happen in any child that experiences a high degree of trauma.

Next time you are talking to a special education teacher, ask them if they have ever worked with a child that was ten years old physically and eight years old emotionally or academically. We experienced this type of child frequently at summer camp for children of prisoners. Here we are, planning our programming around ten to twelve year olds, and we would quickly realize that several kids were eight years old emotionally. This brought to light the importance of having one counselor for every camper. The programming almost needed to be customized for each child who walked onto the ranch.

As a society, when we see a twelve-year-old child, we expect that same child to be emotionally developed as a typical twelve-year-old. But what if these twelve-year-old children who are getting in trouble with the law are really only ten or even eight on the inside? We need to consider what this means for our juvenile laws. We need to consider what this means for our classroom. We need to consider what this means for sex education. We need to consider what this means for future employers and job readiness.

For starters, if our expectations of this child are too high, we get frustrated and they get frustrated. As their frustration increases, their emotional situation is only exacerbated. The result is an outward form of rage, anger, self-harm, or violence of one form or another. Consider this thought again for just a moment: these kids are just trying to communicate with us in the only way they can. They do not have the capacity to do what we are expecting them to do. In other words, the root problem is not with the kids but with the adults. It was the adult environment at home that forced the child into this emotional regression in the first place, and now the expectations of other adults outside the home are only making it worse.

Let me give you an example. I was a guest volunteer at a camp for children of prisoners. The camp had about one counselor for every eight kids. Yes, there were other adults on site that brought the ratio down, but the actual ratio in the cabin at night was too high and too risky. Since I had experience working with the kids, I was put in charge of problem situations, in other words, any fights and violence. It got to the point where I was just going from one situation to another. By the time the camp was over, one child had been in the back of a police car, the fire department and first responders were called, and another child left the camp in an ambulance because of an emotional breakdown. The police had to handcuff one child in order to get some control and after doing so, one of the officers shared with the leaders of the camp they were ill-equipped to run that camp. I think he was right. It was not the kids' fault. It was our problem as adults.

Later one night, I rode with camp leaders in taking a child home because of his violent behavior. That is one of the lowest points in a child's life. He or she does not even have the capacity to attend summer camp or even do the fun things in life without failing.

It was the intent of that camp to help children, but for that child, the camp drove him closer to crime rather than further from it. It was a totally unintended consequence. The people who organized the camp are the greatest people I know, but we are all learning as a society how childhood trauma can completely change a situation.

In an effort to apply what we have learned, we made adjustments to our own camps at Bridge Builders for Kids. We have never sent a child home in the ten years of camping (at our own camps), though there were several that could have been. Johnny was a child that could have been sent home. He came to camp three years in a row.

On the third year, he was becoming a risk to the other kids in camp. At that time we had two sites: the campsite and the ranch site. All the kids loved the ranch site because it had a homey feel to it. There was a dog, several cats, farm animals, horseback riding, hiking, hayrides, and all the things that a secluded ranch away from the big city can provide. The only noise was from the coyotes yipping off the ridges in the distance. The ranch also had two cabins. So here is what we did. Rather than taking Johnny home, we adapted to his situation. We asked Johnny if he would like to spend that night at the ranch in one of the cabins with a couple of adults and no other kids around.

"Really?" he said, "That would be awesome!"

According to the two male adult counselors, as soon as Johnny got into the car, they could feel all the anxiety leave. He was engaging like a normal kid again, and his sorrow was turning to joy. When they arrived at the ranch, they unpacked into the cabin and that night roasted hotdogs in the fire pit under a clear sky of stars. He was now in a controlled environment. Just a few hours earlier, he was ready to *take out* a couple of campers as well as the camp director, and now he had a calm demeanor and excitement in his voice. He had almost no chance of trauma around him, and he had all the positive-adult nurturing he needed. Instead of Johnny experiencing one of the most traumatic times of his life, he may have experienced one of the more enjoyable times of his life.

The message here can be summed up in a couple of sayings: we reap what we sow, and garbage in, garbage out. If we continue to put trauma and neglect into our children as a nation, we will have bad things come back out of our children and our nation. It is as simple as that. Maybe there is nothing wrong with our kids. Consider the possibility that a root problem lies within the adults.

In the next section, we'll see what it looks like when we put time and trauma together.

TIME AND TRAUMA TOGETHER

I was walking down the hall of a rented lodge we were using for family camps. Down the hall a grandmother in her forties was moving along with her grandchild walking behind her. I am not sure if one or both parents of the child were in prison; however, at age eighteen months, both parents had already abandoned the child. The grandmother was not very attentive and barely aware of the circumstances around her. The eighteen-month-old was teetering back and forth behind her and doing everything he could to keep up as he followed behind his grandmother. His hands were stretched upward, and he was calling out to her. She continued walking forward down the hall and then stopped at her room to open the door. This allowed just enough time for the toddler to catch up, only to fall forward and hit his head on the back of her foot as she walked into the room. She never even noticed what happened. The toddler laid face-down on the floor, crying at the top of his lungs. A moment earlier the child was acting in desperation for his grandmother, and now he was in a state of hopelessness as the door slowly swung to a near close. Eventually after a few minutes, the grandmother slowly came back out of the room and took a hold of the crying child's hand and led him into the room and shut the door.

The combined time and trauma issue comes in all shapes and sizes. All too often we saw children at camp who were dealing with both time and trauma issues, not enough positive-adult nurturing, and too much trauma in the home. One of the most unfortunate results of this situation is crime. By the year 2003, I felt compelled to summarize my observations into a theory. As I mentioned earlier, we called it the PAN-time theory. Here is what it said:

PAN-TIME THEORY

A major cause of violent crime is the environment children experience between the ages of zero and ten. The two most specific environmental factors are:

1. Not enough one-to-one positive-adult nurturing (PAN time)

2. Too much trauma

In many instances, there is a combination of both.

My basis was from real-life observations with hundreds of the most at-risk kids. Let me give you a summary of those observations:

- Most six- to eight-year-old children of prisoners are very hungry for attention.

- Many eight- to ten-year-old children of prisoners start to lose that hunger and begin to build protective walls around themselves.

- Many ten- to twelve-year-old children of prisoners are exhibiting behaviors related to crime.

- Several fourteen- to sixteen-year-old children of prisoners have either been in the back seat of a police car or have served some time in a county jail.

The first signs of change often occur prior to the age of ten, which tells us the cause is there too. This would certainly speak to the importance of early childhood education, which I believe to be very positive. However, the focus of the programs is the children. We can keep adding all day every day programs to our children right back to birth, and we will still have the problem. The problem is not with our children. The root problem is with the adults, the self-control and behavior of "we the parents".

I talked to one urban daycare worker who said the first word out the mouth of one of their toddlers was not "Mommy" or "Daddy." The toddler's first words were "F … you." We will never get ahead of this problem by adding more programs for the child. The more effective program is the behavior of the would-be parent. That would change this situation from reactive to proactive in nature. Hopefully, education in positive family structure would result in more stable children growing up in more stable family structures.

STRONGER EVIDENCE

I have identified some supporting evidence, but in my opinion, my argument still needs stronger backing. Is there overwhelming evidence from research that clearly demonstrates the impact of stable fathers and strong family structure being causal to crime? The answer is yes. The proof was articulated in a publication by the Institute for Marriage and Public Policy.[16] iMAPP identified twenty-three U.S. studies published in peer-reviewed journals within a five-year period examining the issue of crime as it relates to family structure. A resounding twenty of the twenty-three studies, or 87 percent, found some family structure effects on crime or delinquency. Of the twenty that found effects, nineteen studies found reduced crime from stronger family structures. In the executive summary, the document states that "married parents appear to reduce both the individual risk and the overall rates of crime."

One featured study in the report drilled down deeper to identify the specific type of marriage being researched. The featured study showed married two-biological-parent families generally fared better than any other family structure examined. As I read through the summaries of each study, the words "married" and "biological" appear to be keys in the more successful structures. One of the limitations in the twenty studies was the use of the phrase "intact." In my opinion, this phrase has the potential of taking on a different meaning in different studies, resulting in a blurring of data.

The specific data used for many of these studies came from the ADD Health Study, which may likely be the most comprehensive research involving adolescent behavior. The research began in 1994 and spanned fourteen years to 2008, involving four waves of questionnaires that revolved around the same group of adolescents coming out of broad and diverse backgrounds.

There is one family structure specifically that we as a nation need to consider as a major contributor to the time and trauma syndrome. We, as adults, keep telling ourselves that out-of-wedlock births are just fine, and they are part of our new family structure in America. However, we need to reeducate ourselves (adults) about this issue. Pure and simple, the math works against this approach. Unless the single parent is rich, the financial resources are cut. The home of this child provides half the nurturing time, half the earning potential, half the economies of scale, half the grandparents, half the extended family. No matter how we do the math, this child comes up short. The economic results are published each year by the U.S. government inside a document called "America's Children—Key National Indicators of Well- Being."[17] Here is a graph from the annual report demonstrating a twenty-seven-year period of time in which roughly half the children growing up in single-mother homes were living in poverty.

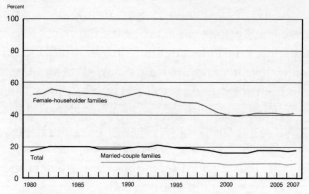

Indicator ECON1.A

Percentage of related children ages 0-17 living a poverty by family structure, 1980-2007

Note: Estimates for related children ages 0-17 include children related to the householder (or reference person of an unrelated subfamily) who are not themselves a householder or spouse of the householder (or family reference person). In 2007, the average poverty threshold for a family of four was $21,203.
SOURCE: U.S. Census Bureau, Current Population Survey, Annual Social and Economic Supplements.

I want to make a personal note here and say that my comments are not a reflection of judgment toward single moms. While spending a decade working with single moms, they would be the first to say they would much prefer a stable marriage rather than dealing with life on their own. In my own life, I was raised by a single mom beginning when I was age ten. I have found single mothers to be heroic in what they can accomplish. However, from a societal perspective, the numbers work against this family structure.

WHAT ABOUT HEALTH?

So, how does this time and trauma issue manifest itself outwardly? The Centers for Disease Control and Prevention (CDC) had this to say in April of 2006:

> Childhood abuse, neglect and exposure to other
> traumatic stressors ... are common. The short-

and long-term outcomes of these childhood exposures include a multitude of health and social problems.[18]

The first thing to note is that neglect and trauma are common. This is not something that is fabricated or exaggerated. The second thing to note is that there are both short- and long-term outcomes. The residual effect can be immediate and persist for a life time. The third item to note is that there are also health issues. So is it just one or two health issues, or is it a multitude of physical health issues? That would really start adding more interest into this issue, wouldn't it? Social issues are one thing, but if this is contributing to the health care costs in America, now we have another whole set of dynamics. Let's take a closer look at a study by the CDC on the issue of time and trauma. This study, called the "ACE Study" (Adverse Childhood Experiences), looked at the impact of abuse, neglect, and family dysfunction that occurs during childhood. The study found that out of 17,000 participants, almost two-thirds reported at least one "ACE." More than one in five reported three or more ACEs.[19]

Here is what the study said about the long-term effects of the abuse and neglect to children:

> The risk of the following *health* problems increases in a strong and graded fashion:
> - alcoholism and alcohol abuse
> - chronic obstructive pulmonary disease
> - depression
> - fetal death
> - health-related quality of life

- illicit drug use
- ischemic heart disease
- liver disease
- risk for intimate partner violence
- multiple sexual partners
- sexually transmitted diseases
- smoking
- suicide attempts
- unintended pregnancies[20]

Let's step back for a moment. Do you see what is going on here? Are you starting to feel the progression that one feels as you start researching this issue?

When I started down this road, I was just looking for the root cause of violent crime, specifically with children of prisoners. Now it is looking more like time and trauma are not only the major factors causing crime; they may likely be the root issues of many of our social issues in America. Instead of stemming just from children of prisoners, this may permeate into other family structures. As I stated earlier, there are certainly middle-class, two-parent families that are seemingly functional from the outside and yet may be experiencing a lack of time or too much trauma on the inside. This problem can affect every type of social or economic class.

Finally, we have been talking about social effects, but do time and trauma affect our government? What I am finding is that PAN time is not only related to criminal justice. It is related to almost every major area of our state and local governments. At the base, it is likely the biggest contributing factor to crime, teen pregnancy, and graduation rates. The biggest influence of PAN time is fatherless homes. At the government level, fatherless homes contribute to the cost of health and human services, education, criminal justice, transportation, safety, real estate tax revenue, FICA contributions, and state and federal income tax revenues. In 2011 we found that state correctional costs are the second-fastest growing expense for state governments.[21]

Wow! Time and trauma prior to age ten stretch wide and go deep. They are root issues. More time and less trauma are what make good family structures work and stressed family structures work better.

THE TRENDS

It is beginning to appear in my mind that time and trauma may be the most significant root causes of at-risk youth. They are big factors in the creation of at-risk youth. Let's summarize it this way: adults are spending less time and invoking more trauma with their children, and this has become the most significant root cause of negative social behaviors of children in the United States today.

Pick out any group of ten youth who have negative social behaviors, and the theory is that one of the biggest contributors will be insufficient time and too much trauma in their home life as a child. Whether it is crime, violent crime, prostitution, teen pregnancy, achievement gap, graduation rates, cutting, drugs, or alcohol, the root cause will include time and trauma at the top of the list.

Whether you consider this a hypothesis or theory or any other term, it is meant to stimulate discussion and debate on this topic. Hopefully, one of the outcomes will be new research confirming a causal relationship between time and trauma before age ten and negative social behaviors later in life. Efforts in this area will move the thought process from a theory to something with a higher level of credibility and with more empirical data. In the meantime, I will work with the data we have and piece it together in an organized manner, a meta-analysis of sorts.

With this in mind, a common question arises. What are the trends? The trends will cause you to lean forward in your chair as we look closer. In this section, I will answer this question along with the resulting social impact.

I will start by using numbers from different sources of research and organize them in a grid or chart. Secondly, I will apply the time and trauma theory to these numbers. Do you think it is possible to project whether an eight-year-old will own a home someday or graduate from high school? Let's try simulating a chart that would give us those projections. The process I worked through to develop this chart can be found in the back of the book. For our purposes today let's see it as part of the PAN-time theory. The purpose of the chart is to help us understand the full effects of the PAN-time theory and family structure. Take a moment to look at the PAN-time theory chart. Please keep in mind it is not from one source of research. It is a broad approach only and simply gives credibility to a theory.

PAN-TIME THEORY CHART

Input			Output		
Hours of Nurturing/ per Day per Child	Crime %	Grad %	Welfare %	Employ %	Home Own %
3-4	2	90	3	95	67
2-3	19	85	9	NA	NA
1-2	36	65	18	76	27
0-1	55	45	36	62	5

Let me explain the chart. The hours represented in the left column are hours of nurturing in the home. Just as a reminder, an hour of nurturing is determined by the time given to a child by an adult in their home on a one-to-one basis or equivalent. It is assumed that a high degree of trauma in the home can cause a child to drop down in the grid by .5 hours per day. It would not surprise me if further research found the trauma impact to be more severe, but for now we will lean to the smaller impact.

As you may remember, children growing up on the farm one hundred years ago (John Boy Walton) likely received four to five hours per day of nurturing time. This category is not even listed in the grid. At the bottom of the grid, there are no negative numbers, even though children with a negative time score actually showed up in our research. These were children who were not receiving any one-to-one nurturing and had significant trauma in the home.

Next, I will speculate on where our society currently would line up in this grid. Again, this is only my opinion, and the chart is shown to help us understand the value of more research.

PAN-TIME THEORY CHART

Input	Output				
Hours of Nurturing/ per Day per Child	Crime %	Grad %	Welfare %	Employ %	Home Own %
3-4	2	90	3	95	67
2-3	19	85	9	NA	NA
1-2	36	65	18	76	27
0-1	55	45	36	62	5

------- Line indicates estimated current nurturing and resulting social outcomes in America.

Now let's talk about the trend of this line and where we are headed in the future.

If the information from the *American Psychologist* described earlier in the chapter is extrapolated over twenty years, it is possible that children in America have dropped one hour of nurturing per day over the last two decades. This means that over the last twenty years, the average child has dropped down one full row in the above grid. If this is actually happening, it would help explain why our prison population doubled from 1990 to 2000 and continues to grow rapidly. It would help explain a major cause of our achievement gap. It would help explain the source of many of our welfare recipients. It would give us some understanding of the problem with workforce readiness. It would also give us some indicators of future homeownership.

Fatherless home trends are consistent with this chart as well. If we extrapolate fatherless home trends from the last five years forward twenty years, they would double as well, which would bring us to 80 percent of babies being born without a committed father.

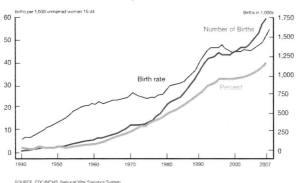

Figure 1. Number of births, birth rate, and percentage of births to unmarried women: United States, 1940-2007

SOURCE: CDC/NCHS, National Vital Statistics System.

The possible trends of time and trauma and fatherless family structures are the most worrisome part of this whole issue and chapter. If I were giving you a verbal presentation right now, this is where my voice would get louder and my passion would get stronger. If the average child in America continues to drop one hour of nurturing every twenty years, what does that do for our society and our economy? We are not sure of the full ramifications. But what if the table is close to reality? Take a look at the grid again and see what implications you would see if we drop one box in the next twenty years! What does it mean for crime and police? What does it mean for education in the U.S.? What does it mean for our ability to compete with China or Japan in twenty years? We do not know the rate of fatherless homes in China, but Japan has a 2 percent rate of fatherless homes according to a May 2009 report from the CDC.[23] It's not 40 percent like America but 2 percent. The nation with the highest percent of fatherless homes is Iceland at 66 percent, and they went bankrupt in 2008. I am not saying the fatherless rate in Iceland caused the bankruptcy, but I am relatively certain it did not help.

What do these trends mean for tax revenues into our state and federal government? What does it mean for real estate taxes for our local government? It is almost a little hard to imagine. As I write this, I am questioning the idea myself, and then as I look at the bottom row of the grid, I remember that there is a large population of youth in every major urban city in the U.S. that already has graduation rates of 50 percent. Many of those same children have a 50 percent chance of getting involved with crime. It brings me back to the children I worked with at camp at the beginning of this chapter and hearing of them being arrested as they get older.

What concerns me most is the social damage that could occur from the next hour of nurturing that we lose. As a nation, we are coping with and adapting to the social damage from the last hour of nurturing that we lost. Will the next hour of nurturing that we lose as a society have an equal amount of social damage, or will the damage grow exponentially? We can cope with one out of ten, but at what point does it start to crack the foundation of our social structure?

We have seen exponential growth in other areas of our society. In the 1960s, health care consumed 5 percent of our economy. Today it costs 17 percent of our economy.[24] Does our economy have the ability to wring out more dollars for additional social programs?

As a nation we have had a strong economy for much of the last twenty years. We have been able to absorb the cost with little attention. What happens if the economy slows down in growth compared to the last twenty years?

I want to be careful at this point in the book not to sound the alarm too early in the process. However, at the same time, our society is not showing any signs of slowing down the time and trauma trend. Out-of-wedlock birthrates continue to rise. A CDC report in early 2008 showed that 25 percent of teen girls between the ages of fourteen and nineteen have at least one STD.[25] This is astounding! Does this make anyone else want to stand up and shout, "Stop this social train; it isn't working"?

The considerations grow even worse. What percent of these teenage girls will end up with cervical cancer? How many will become sterile? What societal impact occurs if these numbers continue to increase? Therefore, I think the alarm does need to be activated even for the purpose of public awareness of our current situation. The issue needs to get on the table and be dealt with by our society. Based on the numbers and if trends continue, my prediction is this: *it is likely 25 percent of babies born today will either be arrested or have an unwanted pregnancy by age eighteen.* This will come at a time when 20 percent of our population is made up of senior citizens.[26] This scenario puts a lot of pressure on working-age adults to move this nation forward in a tough, competitive global economy. We have to deal with our own national lack of self-control and behavior as adults. We have to deal with root issues, or they will deal with us.

Calculated support for my prediction above is included in the back of the book if you enjoy the detail.

Now let's take a look at the financial cost in the next section.

THE COST

In the previous section, we talked about trends and the future. In this section we will go back and just look at the cost of fatherless homes in our nation today. So, let's dive into this question.

As I said in the first section of this chapter, I believe that fatherless homes (time and trauma) may likely cost 1 to 5 percent of our nation's economy. For easy figuring, let's assume the gross domestic product in the U.S. is $14 trillion.[27] One percent of $14 trillion is $140 billion.

I have included the calculations used to determine the annual costs of fatherlessness in the back of the book. I did not want to take the risk of someone falling asleep at this point in the chapter. Let's look at the five social areas used in the PAN-time chart and the *estimated* costs related to fatherless homes. I italicized "estimated" because again, due to the lack of research and attention to root issues, we have some calculations of our own. The most accurate data came from estimating three of the five areas from the charts. They were crime, welfare, and employment. Those three social costs alone deriving from fatherless homes would amount to $224 billion per year in the nation. It would be easy to predict that these areas alone could amount to 1 to 2 percent of the nation's economy.

What about other social areas not considered? Many of the children who are experiencing low time or high trauma may be the first to post compromising pictures of themselves on Myspace or Facebook. Here is a shocker for you. At a congressional hearing in the fall of 2007, our nation's leaders listened to testimony on the role of the Internet in producing home-grown terrorists. The name for this process is radicalization. One testimony suggested that terrorist recruiters actually scanned these websites, profiling vulnerable youth as prospects for recruitment into terrorist organizations.[28] Wow! This set me back in my chair as I listened to this concept. Are the youth of our generation strong enough in themselves to resist these cunning attempts to lure them in? Have we instilled in them strong self-images? As the parent of two former teenagers, I have a hard time even including this type of concept in this book. It's scary.

All things considered in the social areas of time and trauma, 2 to 3 percent of our economy could be a fair estimate, although even further consideration should be given to the thousands of nonprofits across the nation in the private sector that focus resources on many of these areas. Giving U.S.A reports that Americans donated $303.8 billion to charity in 2009.[29] Certainly a significant portion of those dollars are provided for children with little time and too much trauma. Charitable giving would further bolster a 2 to 3 percent cost.

The last thing I will mention is health. The CDC report called ACE includes a long list of potential adult health issues from childhood neglect and trauma.[30] Is it possible the health issues can double our cost of fatherless homes in America to 5 percent of our GDP?

In the end, what does it really cost to neglect our youth? More than we can afford.

THE SOLUTIONS

Are you ready for a key point in the book? Are we ready to apply the information from chapters one and two? Let's diagnose and distinguish the surface issues from the root issues in crime.

EXAMPLES OF SURFACE SOLUTIONS
More Prisons

Adding more prisons equates to treating the symptom. I am not suggesting we stop building prisons. We need more in the short run. Long term, they do not fix the problem.

More Early Childhood Programs

Adding more early childhood programs equates to treating the symptom. I am not saying we should stop feeding kids free lunches at school or stop the pre-K programs. We need them in the short run. However, long term they do not fix the problem.

EXAMPLE OF A ROOT SOLUTION
Parental Behavior

The only individual who can control the amount of time and trauma in a child's life is the parent. Decreasing fatherless homes and increasing functional two-parent homes is the root solution for this chapter.

ROOT STRATEGIES FOR OUR SC

Before we start talking about individual solut.
must set a goal or objective. You may not agree w.
goal. However, even if you agree with any part o.
goal, I welcome your enthusiasm. Here is the socie.al
goal, and it is a very simple concept. We want every
person to progress through these three steps in order.

Goal: Get our three steps in order:

1. Education

2. Marriage

3. Children

We need to encourage this order in life. The benefits of focusing on education first are clear. Marriage
can come quickly or not so quickly after education, and
then third comes children.

This order will allow for the best chance of ranking
number one among nations again in education. This
order will allow for simpler marriages. This order will
allow for healthier and more successful children. Now,
I am not saying this has to be exact; that is unrealistic. I
am saying this from a general perspective. My own son,
Ben, graduated from college and then married his wife,
Nicole, while she was in her second year of medical
school. In this case, education was generally first.

I want to break away for a minute and have a sidebar
discussion. Let's imagine for a moment that everyone
you know has followed this chronological order. You in
your own personal life followed this order. You completed your education; next you got married; and next

you had children. You and your spouse followed the order. If this was true, and I came to you and stated this order is part of our core values as a society, likely 90 percent of you would agree (just guessing). There is no problem. But now that each of us has friends and family members who have not followed this order, we are less inclined to agree so readily. Why? Because we do not want to offend the people around us. We do not want to offend the people we love. Here is where we need to stop for a minute. If what I just described is true, then we have to be careful not to allow behavior (on a macro level) to drive our core values as a society. Isn't that what just happened? Instead we need to properly separate this out into two issues:

1. First, maintain our core values in their proper place as we discussed in chapter two.

2. Second, love and not judge our friends and family who have allowed the order to change in their life.

Too often as a society we confuse ourselves and think we are only capable of one of the two. I think we are sophisticated enough to do both. If we allow our behavior to drive our core values, we are no different than the politicians and negative advertising. If we change the bedrock in any way, the future will likely result in destruction.

The trend today is to begin sexual activity in the middle of high school education. Many times this results in unwanted pregnancies. This is getting us out of order. If our society embraces the trend of three, two, one, or children, marriage, education, then our success as a society will be limited, to say the least.

It is my personal belief that if a child is born in the U.S. with a mother and father at their side and receives a good education, then that child has as much potential as *anyone* on this earth.

It is also my belief that a child born in the U.S. with a mother and father at their side will have a tremendously positive effect on society. If we have a daddy in every doorway, we don't need a cop on every corner.

It is funny that our appreciation for this order becomes even stronger when we have tried life in a different order.

So, how do we even begin to turn around a social trend that is headed in the wrong direction? It is a difficult task. Let's list out some strategies that might get us on track with education first, marriage second, and children third.

My hope is that if our public learns more about this issue, the public will turn itself around in the same way education of smoking turned our direction around.

So, what area specifically do we focus our attention on? I have always been a fan of being proactive versus reactive. This will generally lead us to the most effective resolutions. Let me focus on encouraging the parents that are reading this book.

If you are a parent and you want grandkids after your kids are married, please take this seriously. Parents feel they are losing the battle with peer influence and today's culture. However, do not lose heart, parents. The June/July 2003 article in the *American Psychologist* says that " ... positive parent-child relationships, parental supervision and consistent discipline, and communication of family values are the major reasons youth do not engage in delinquent or unhealthy behaviors."[31] So be encouraged, parents. We can do it!

ENCOURAGEMENT FOR PARENTS
Parents of Preschoolers

Set a goal of providing *one thousand to two thousand hours per year* of nurturing per child in your home. This does not have to be very scientific. It comes down to roughly three to six hours per day. If there are two parents and two children in your home and you spend three hours at the kitchen table a day, you are halfway there.

- If you have a two-parent home and you are not even close to the goal, one of the parents may need to consider being at home with your children. It will be the noblest thing you can do. It builds a strong America.

- If you are around *one thousand hours per year,* and you absolutely cannot have one parent at home, consider some viable alternatives:

  1. Find a favorite grandparent, relative or neighbor who can come to your house one day a week to be with your kids, even if you have to pay the relative or neighbor. This will provide the nurturing and reduce any trauma by keeping the child in the safety and comfort of their home.

2. Send your child to the home of the relative or neighbor, as long as there are not already ten to twenty kids in that home.

3. If you use a daycare, find one that has a similar feel to the child's home and with a low ratio of children to adults.

4. In any of the scenarios above, I cannot emphasize enough the importance of sitting with your preschool child close to you and reading books. This has an obvious positive impact on their emotional and mental nurturing.

Parents of School-Aged Children

Set a goal of providing one thousand hours per year of nurturing per child in your home. This does not have to be real scientific. It comes down to roughly three hours per day. If there are two parents and two children in your home and you spend three hours at the kitchen table a day, you are already there. Similar to the preschool parent, here are some considerations:

• If you have a two-parent home and you are not even close to the goal, one of the parents may need to consider being at home with your children.

• If you are close to your goal and you absolutely cannot have one parent at home, consider some viable alternatives:

1. Find a job for one parent to work only during the hours the kids are in school.

2. Find a job for one of the parents that allows that parent to be off with the kids during the summer if the kids do not have summer school.

Parents of Teenagers

Don't give up. Stay engaged and available to your teenagers. Be encouraged! You may think the rolling eyes and hurried conversations on the way out the door are a reason for discouragement, but they are not. You will survive. In terms of your teen, studies show that the *parent-child relationship* is still the major reason youth will avoid unhealthy behavior. Even if you have a teen who is already involved in unhealthy behaviors, this applies to you and maybe even more. Don't give up; stay in there! Your unconditional love over the long haul will prevail.

If your teenager is not yet sexually active, I do want to carefully bring up the issue of abstinence during high school. I know there is a debate over the effectiveness of abstinence education, and you may have all the research lined up against abstinence education. Abstinence is the only one hundred percent effective means against sexually transmitted diseases and unwanted pregnancies. Our kids really need to hear all the risks and considerations before engaging in sexual activity. One government study called the ADD Study showed that teenagers who are abstinent in their teen years are nearly twice as likely to graduate from college.[32] If our culture is truly interested in the education of our youth, we have to be talking about abstinence at least in the home. The same study showed that abstaining teenagers will earn $370,000 more money over their lifetime then teenagers who are sexually active. Our teenagers need to know the truth.

Please allow me to talk a bit more about abstinence. As someone who spent ten years putting together budgets, this issue comes down to numbers. If you can peel away the cultural and political trends and just look at numbers, abstinence with our teenagers and having children after marriage cannot be beat numerically. We cannot argue with the numbers. Abstinence always works, and children after marriage will provide more resources for our children from day one. The debatable issue is the "education" part in abstinence education. If we do not teach abstinence within the school curriculum, there is nothing wrong with establishing that expectation and providing that education in the home. But how do we clearly communicate to our teenagers at the secondary level? Are there other ways of approaching the subject?

I was a guest speaker in a classroom of high school teenagers. I was speaking on the abundant opportunities available to young adults in America. My specific area was global careers and working in other nations. I asked what income level they wanted to achieve by age forty. Many of the students said $150,000. I told them it is entirely possible for that to happen. However, it will not happen without discipline and sacrifice. I told

CHAPTER 4

them one of the requirements of foreign workers in the U.S. government is a medical clearance. Being sexually active when they are in high school only increases the risk of failing that clearance. Then it got really quiet in the room. They seemed hungry to have an honest discussion about this topic. So, I went further and asked the question, "Can I just share something with you right now?" They all nodded their heads and were fully focused. I responded with these words: "It is okay to be a virgin when you graduate from high school," and then I repeated the statement. You could just feel the mood in the room. There was an atmosphere and desire to have a deep conversation about this topic. They were very receptive to hear someone else's perspective. There may have been several students that really needed that encouragement and needed a noble reason *not* to be sexually active. Many of them received that noble reason; they really wanted to focus on their career and did not want to risk compromising their future. I am sure there were also hormone-filled students that thought, *Darn. There goes my chance for tonight.*

THOUGHTS FOR POLICY MAKERS
In our pursuit of happiness, let us not forget the obvious.

1. Access to College

    My observation in working with all types of youth is this: the number-one reason teenagers consider college is because someone in their household expects them to go to college. Having two parents in the household increases the likelihood of that expectation. What is the cost of the extra encouragement from a functional two-parent home to the American taxpayer? Zero.

2. Access to Children's Health Care

The best access to health care for children is access to a functional mother and father. If you doubt this even a bit, refer back to the CDC study called ACE. What are the results of childhood neglect and trauma? The answer is: alcoholism and alcohol abuse, chronic obstructive pulmonary disease, depression, fetal death, health-related quality of life, illicit drug use, ischemic heart disease, liver disease, risk for intimate partner violence, multiple sexual partners, sexually transmitted diseases, smoking, suicide attempts, and unintended pregnancies.[33] Remember also this is information from the federal government. So, what is the cost for the functional two-parent home to the American taxpayer? Zero.

3. Reducing Children in Poverty

The best approach to reducing children in poverty is a two-parent home. Two-parent homes average more household income than single-parent homes experience. It is simply a matter of math. What is the cost for the functional two-parent home to the American taxpayer? Zero.

4. Reducing Youth and Gang Violence

The best approach to reducing the number of children involved in violent behavior is a two-parent home. The Texas Department of Justice reports that 85 percent of all youth in prison come from fatherless homes.[34] Continue to look at the research I provided earlier in the chapter, and it will be easy to determine that the best way to decrease youth violence is by promoting family structures with married, biological parents. What is the cost for the functional two-parent home to the American taxpayer? Zero.

5. Reduce the Achievement Gap in America's Youth

Research shows that children who receive more one-to-one nurturing (even fifty hours per year more) are 53 percent less likely to skip school and 37 percent less likely to skip class.[35] What is the cost for a functional two-parent home to the American taxpayer? Zero.

Well, you get the picture. These five thoughts now beg the question, "Who is responsible to promote a functional two-parent home?" We will get to that in Chapter Nine.

CONCLUSION

Remember the story I told about the toddler whose first words were "F... you"? In an uncanny way, that toddler may be a valid spokesperson for our youngest generation. That toddler may have communicated as clearly as possible to our nation's adults that things are not going very well with his generation. Will we listen?

The purpose of this chapter is to understand a root cause of crime. A root cause of crime is a behavior, and that specific adult behavior is this: we are not spending enough time with our children, and we allow our children to experience too much trauma. This scenario is more prevalent in homes absent of married biological parents. Fatherless family structures are the largest contributor to this scenario. What is especially concerning are the trends of fatherless homes in the U.S. and what that means for us as a nation if we do not consider the root issues that are calling out.

In chapter five, we will introduce a root cause of a root cause of crime as case study #3. You may have never heard of this root issue. I found it to be fascinating information. After you read the next chapter, you will be telling your friends about it.

ROOT LESSON FROM CHAPTER FOUR:

If we have a daddy in every doorway, we don't need a cop on every corner.

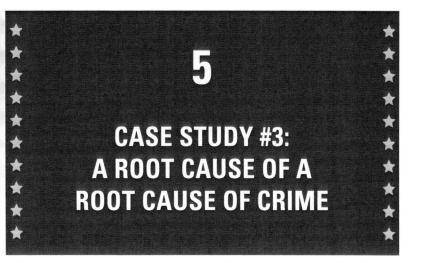

5

CASE STUDY #3:
A ROOT CAUSE OF A
ROOT CAUSE OF CRIME

It was a hot day, and it was hard to find a breeze any-where. Being stuck in a county fair booth for any amount of time just does not pay enough. Next time a local judge sentences a first-time offender, it should include community service and three days staffing a county fair booth. It was time to get out and look around a bit. I had no idea I was going to stumble on to someone who would totally challenge my thinking about the root cause of crime.

I was at the Blue Earth County fairgrounds near Mankato, Minnesota, where a gentleman by the name of Jody Allen Crowe also had a fair booth. He would be the one to show me that root issues can be like walk-ing through a cave. One cave can lead to a string of more caves. Not wanting to get stuck in a long con-versation, I stood back away from his booth, trying to gather as much information as possible without mak-ing eye contact. In Minnesota, there is something called "Minnesota Nice." It is fairly self-explanatory and often includes saying hi when you make eye contact at a small-town venue.

After feeling more confident his fair booth was someplace I would risk stopping at for a few minutes, I approached Mr. Crowe. Nearly an hour later, we were still talking about crime prevention. I was fascinated to find out Mr. Crowe is the author of a book that describes the root issue of school shootings across America. It is called *The Fatal Link*. What was even more fascinating was his assessment of my theory on time and trauma that I described to you in chapter four: "Your root issue is correct, but it does not go deep enough."

"What?" I said.

How can you go back further than zero years of age in a child's life to find a root cause? Is that possible? Was my theory on time and trauma just the entrance cave? The only person that can articulate the answer is Mr. Crowe himself. He is my second of three Minnesota friends who will guest-contribute to this book. I will let him speak to you directly in the rest of this chapter. I will be back at the end of the chapter.

AMERICA'S GREATEST BRAIN DRAIN

"This is a Fox News alert! Nine people are now reported dead in a mass shooting in a shopping mall in Omaha, Nebraska."

In 2008, I watched as another unexplained, tragically violent act was being played out on the television screen. The nineteen-year-old shooter, in what was described as Nebraska's worst mass shooting ever, was portrayed as a troubled youth. His father had, at one time, asked police to arrest him to "scare him straight." He had lost his job at McDonalds for stealing money. He had been treated for ADD and ADHD and depression, and had dropped out of school. His suicide note stated he wanted to go out with style.

I listened and watched to see if anyone asked the question or explored the possibility of prenatal exposure to alcohol. I saw the same television experts espousing behaviors and motives but not the root cause. I heard one police officer state that it may be impossible to come up with an explanation. Ask me. I will ask the burning question! Please, please, please, ask the question!

I am an educator who has worked for eighteen years in the epicenters of prenatal exposure to alcohol on reservations across the country. During that time, I studied the research into the brain damage that occurs from prenatal exposure to alcohol that shows up in lowered academic ability, higher levels of conduct disorders, violence, promiscuous behaviors, early drug and alcohol use, depression, suicides, and physical malformations up to and including death. Most of the students I worked with were victims of prenatal exposure to alcohol. I had to know what worked, so I studied the research. I wanted to provide the optimal educational experience for our students.

The research is clear and unequivocal. Alcohol is a powerful teratogen. The root word for teratogen is the Greek word, *tera*, meaning monster. A teratogen is defined as an agent capable of causing serious harm to the fetus. Lead is also a powerful teratogen. Alcohol and lead are the only two teratogens a woman could ingest that kill the brain cells of the fetus. Women drink alcohol, not lead. Because alcohol causes central nervous system damage, it is also classified as a neurobehavioral teratogen. This cannot be said often enough; alcohol is a teratogen and as such is much more damaging to the brain than meth, cocaine, or crack.[36]

Bluntly said, a woman's drinking during pregnancy damages the brain. Damaged brains do not function like normal brains. Damaged brains cause people to do things a normal person would not do. Currently, up to 40 percent[37] of our children, and in some locations, up to 50 percent,[38] are born prenatally exposed to alcohol, anywhere from a drink or two a week to heavy daily drinking.

The brain of the fetus is damaged many ways. Individual brain cells die, neurons are damaged, and cells migrate to the wrong locations. The white brain cells that make up the brain message centers are particularly susceptible to damage. Lowered IQ and slower brain speed are evidence of the damage. Research continues to confirm ethanol in the alcohol is the culprit. Longitudinal studies confirm the brain damage is irreversible.

In most everyone's mind, for an individual to have a fetal alcohol syndrome, the person must have the *look* (and even then, few recognize the syndrome). The *look* is that of the classic, heavily impacted Fetal Alcohol Syndrome (FAS) child. The birth defects of FAS include lowered IQ, small stature, small head, slack muscles, lack of the defined structure between the nose and lip, called the philtrum, a thin upper lip, epicanthal folds between the eye and nose, causing the appearance of almond-shaped eyes and a greater distance between the eyes than normal, other facial anomalies, heart problems, kidney problems, hair growth on the back of the neck, genital deformities, eye problems, shortened and/or bent fingers, hip deformities, pigeon or concave chest, cleft palate, spinal dimple, and/or hernias.[39]

FAS children, affected by the resulting brain damage, are obviously expected to be lower functioning and usually receive services through the schools and other human services (without officially recognizing that the child is a victim of the syndrome).

But FAS is only the tip of the iceberg. By far, the greater share of brain-damaged individuals do not have any facial characteristics. Fetal Alcohol Spectrum Disorder (FASD)[40] is not a diagnosis, but rather a way to describe the exhibitions of brain damage from prenatal exposure to alcohol that is evident without any physical deformity. Since there is no diagnosis for prenatal exposure to alcohol in the *Diagnostic and Statistical Manual* used by psychologists and psychiatrists, psychologists and psychiatrists do not diagnose as FASD.[41] The behaviors are classified under some other labels, many of which are typically medicated.

I have found very few professionals who understand or have taken the time to learn that the physical syndrome features of FASD are only a small part of the entire spectrum. The victims of prenatal exposure to alcohol who have none of the classic syndrome features are the kids who are at great risk because we think they should behave and think normally because they look normal.

The warnings are there. Every alcohol container warns of the dangers. Every woman who drinks while pregnant is walking a tightrope of chance. She may think she can make it through with no damage to the child, but one binge, one time where a couple beers are drunk quickly without food in her stomach, one or two glasses of wine a day to calm the nerves, a family occasion, a wedding party, a night out with the girls, and she falls off that tightrope without knowing the damage that is happening to the little life inside.

Her baby looks so perfect, has all the fingers and toes, a full head of hair, and so seemingly fine. Not until first grade, when the child struggles with linking a sound to a symbol, or has trouble sounding out a three-letter word while the rest of the class is moving on to consonant blends, will the truth be known. She won't know until the temper tantrums escalate, or the impulsive behaviors impede learning, or her child's inability to attend to a task brings calls from the teacher. That perfect-looking child will then reveal the brain damage from that one binge, that party, that forgotten weekend, or those two glasses of wine a day. And, if our awareness of this silent epidemic does not change, the culprit will remain hidden behind the cloak of ignorance.

The greatest dilemma is the fact that much of the brain damage occurs without any physical deformities. The child looks perfect, with symmetry to the face and body and no indication of the atrophy of the brain. This hidden damage is fooling professionals and parents. A shield of ignorance, almost impenetrable due to the unwillingness to confront the truth, protects the alcohol industry. We are condemning another generation of unborn with the message that only massive drinking causes harm. If you don't see the damage, no harm done. Wrong.

The time between conception and the realization of being pregnant exposes 25 percent to 30 percent of fetuses to alcohol.[42] Women who would never drink if they knew they were pregnant unwittingly can damage the fetus to the point of the full syndrome because they don't know they are pregnant.

A professional woman engaged me in a conversation in a church basement. She knew I spoke on FASD. Here was someone you would never think would drink while pregnant, a well-respected professional in every way, knowledgeable about the dangers of drinking while pregnant, and working with children who exhibited behaviors reflective of prenatal exposure.

She confided to me her story of an unplanned pregnancy and the social drinking she was doing with her husband and friends prior to finding out about her pregnancy. She spoke of her shock upon finding out she was pregnant and her concerns for her child. This is a common story, unplanned pregnancy and drinking during child-bearing years. We need more than education, but will more education stop this dilemma?

Adopted children, unfortunately, are at a very high risk of having been prenatally exposed to alcohol.[43] American families, to avoid adopting a crack baby from the United States, many times have adopted undetected brain-damaged FASD children from Romania, Bulgaria, and other Middle European countries. The unsuspecting adoptive parents are then overwhelmed with the litany of problems as a result of the biological mother's drinking that led to brain damage. Simply put, who are the mothers who abandon their babies or put their babies up for adoption? The vast majority are young mothers who don't want or can't take care of their babies. These unborn children are at great risk of being the victims of binge drinking by the young mothers.

I have also worked with enough prenatally exposed children to know some have exceptional intelligence along with lack of judgment, lack of impulse control, and/or other behaviors of brain damage. Many times, some of the brain damage behaviors are masked by medication. Researchers have documented FASD victims scoring 120 on IQ tests.[44] They also have scored outside the norm on behavioral scales. The ethanol in the alcohol does not choose what damage to do; the amount and timing of exposure creates the opportunity for the ethanol to do its damage. A child exposed one time with one binge, at a certain time during the pregnancy, may only suffer brain damage exhibited by lack of judgment, lack of a conscience, depression, or limited impulse control while maintaining a high level of intelligence. This deceptive damage hides behind our society's hesitancy to accept prenatal exposure to alcohol as a real problem. We prefer to medicate and call that the cure.

Understandably, teachers have historically not accepted FASD-linked conduct disorder behaviors in schools. The result leaves an FASD victim, whose behaviors are a result of something they had limited or no control over, looking for acceptance among adults with limited or no success. When that acceptance is not found, the secondary disabilities of FASD take control. Secondary disabilities are, among others, depression, disrupted school experience, trouble with the law, confinement or foster placement, inappropriate sexual behaviors, and mental health problems, drug and alcohol use, and exposure to violence.[45]

A typical middle school, junior high school, or high school setting with expectations of increased internal controls and increased maturity is not a benign environment for the FASD brain. The FASD brain is emotionally and socially immature, living in a world that expects it to act and think its age.

Many times adults, teachers, and parents are shaming and blaming the victim for behaviors associated with FASD without realizing they are compounding the problem. Many of these children suffer from threats, punishment, and are exposed to abuse. Many of the parents have FASD themselves and struggle with parenting skills. The FASD child needs structure to be successful. Many have structure only at school, and that structure may only have punitive responses that do not work for the FASD brain.

These conditions bring on the secondary disabilities of FASD. FASD brain dysfunction leads to depression and brings on alcohol and drug use, a behavior shared by the majority of FASD adolescents. This victim will continue to fall further behind in school and eventually leave the mainstream or completely leave school when forced to take academic courses that are completely outside the realm of possible success. Impulsive actions bring punitive discipline but with little or no resulting change of behavior. In many cases, the illogical male FASD brain reacts violently to the punitive action. This results in more secondary disabilities, including a disrupted school experience or a record with law enforcement. Anger and frustration are visible signs of the secondary disabilities. With few exceptions, psychologists and psychiatrists will analyze the behaviors of the FASD victim evidenced by the secondary disabilities of depression, anger, and violence and diagnose a mental illness without any acknowledgement or understanding of *the real root cause*, prenatal exposure to alcohol.

Two sixth-grade students in one of my schools were roughhousing while waiting for the bus. As does many times happen, their seemingly harmless antics flared to anger and quickly erupted into stone throwing. Both boys were from families that were alcohol-involved, and both had the resulting behaviors of FASD. A rock hit a window, shattering the glass. As their teacher, I was at the scene within seconds and interrupted the action, taking both boys to the office.

Once inside the office, one of the boys quickly agreed he was responsible. The other exploded into violence, smashing anything close. As his temper subsided, both the principal and I explained how both were equally responsible for throwing rocks, even though only one of them threw the rock that hit the window.

I left the office and was walking across the campus when the boy who thought he was unjustly punished came rushing up to me, his face twisted in anger. I put out my hand to stop him, trying to reason with him and giving him the opportunity to vent his anger toward me. I was completely unprepared for the roundhouse right fist that landed on my left ear. His brain had acted impulsively when throwing rocks, and had been unable or unwilling to accept the consequence, and had acted violently toward me with no thought to the consequence of his action. The only thing that saved me was the fact he was not using something lethal in his attack.

Many people with a normal brain use a fantasy world to cope with reality. Fads such as wannabe gang involvement, Goth, with the influences from nineteenth-century Gothic literature and horror movies, Hitler, Myspace virtual worlds, manifestos, video games, and fad clothing are mechanisms for the brain to escape from reality or to search for common interests. A normal brain can sort out what is reality and what is fantasy. A normal brain can play a violent video game and understand the fantasy. A normal brain can get deeply involved in Goth or video games without the fantasy becoming reality. An FASD brain does not have the same capability. The fantasy becomes interwoven into their reality.

All adolescents are influenced by their peers. Group behaviors are well documented, and mob mentality is shown on television quite frequently. The FASD brain is influenced in ways a normal brain can resist. Many times, I have witnessed FASD adolescents being goaded into violent behaviors by their peers who knew they could get their dirty work done by these students. Among our staff, we would refer to some of our students as the *bazooka*. Other kids would point the *bazooka* at someone they wanted to harm and pull the trigger by convincing them of the need to fight. The *bazooka* would go off with violent results. Many FASD brains live for the adrenalin rush of action, the acceptance of peers, and the excitement of the fight. When the FASD brain starts to fixate on the solution and begins telling others of his plan, his closest friends, most likely with some of the same brain characteristics, thrive on encouraging him to engage in the violent behaviors, a factor that is hard for the FASD brain to overcome.

The professionals working with children exhibiting the behaviors of brain damage need to learn and understand the root cause. Professionals need to move past the fear of embarrassing or shaming the mother. They need to move past unsubstantiated denials of drinking in order to make an accurate diagnosis of the behaviors exhibited by the child and, in my opinion, to realize how much this is impacting our society. I have long since stopped worrying if I am making the parents feel guilty by asking the question. I have actually found the opposite to be true. Mothers and fathers have been relieved to find out the root cause and have requested more information.

Psychologists and doctors make a mistake that contributes to the dilemma. Many make the assumption the behaviors of the child are genetically passed from the parents. Parents explain they had the same characteristics when they were a child. In my experience, the parents were explaining their own FASD behaviors. No one thought to ask them if the parents' mothers drank. The behaviors thought to be genetic are, in many or most cases, evidence of the generation after generation of brain damage caused by prenatal exposure to alcohol.

For many years working on reservations, I thought I was working where the abnormal had become normal, where children with brain damage were the norm rather than children with healthy brains. I now see we are all living where the abnormal has become normal. Our entire society has been impacted with this epidemic to the extent we think it is normal that 30 percent or more of our children will have problems with reading and math. We think violence and crime are normal. We think it is normal when one out of five children have mental illness, depression, and are medicated with Ritalin and other psychotropic drugs. This is not normal. We live where the abnormal has become normal!

Brain damage from prenatal exposure to alcohol is not a respecter of ethnic, religious, or geographic boundaries. Our judicial system is full of men and women who have this damage.[46] Our schools are overwhelmed with the challenges brought to their doors by children with this little understood brain damage. Our education system is reeling with the expectations of success that will never be met for students with this brain damage. Adult FASD males are swamping the judicial system. Adult FASD females are flooding the social services system with entire families of FASD children and unwanted or uncared-for brain-damaged babies. Teenage FASD girls are having unwanted and unplanned pregnancies, exposing their children at alarming rates. Teenage boys are committing violent acts that are clogging the juvenile systems and putting many of them in adult courts due to the nature of the violence. Adoptive babies are overwhelmingly

FASD and are costing our society billions of dollars.[47] As is said in the FAS community, "The
girls get knocked up; the boys get locked up."

Our country's FASD population is growing at an exponential rate. In my experience, it
was common to see four, five, and six children
in the same family with two, three, and four
or more different fathers. These children were
prenatally exposed to alcohol and struggling
immensely in school. Within fifteen years,
the children were having families of their own
and prenatally exposing them to alcohol, many
times abandoning them to grandmothers and
the foster system. The vicious cycle continues,
adding more FASD children every generation.

One evening I watched MSNBC's *The Mind
of Manson*, a documentary detailing the horrific
murders committed by Charles Manson and
his band of followers. The program was filled
with his lifelong illogical rantings which continued whenever he was in front of a camera
or in front of a parole board. As I watched, I
wondered if he was another person whose brain
was *wired wrong* because of prenatal exposure
to alcohol.

An FBI profiler added comment throughout the MSNBC magazine show, bringing the
psychological profiling expertise of the highly
regarded federal law-enforcement agency to the
table in the discussion of why Manson did what
he did. Her final statement was profoundly
wrong. She said the home environment shaped
the criminal brain. "Occasionally," she said,

"there is a bad seed." She completely missed the most important piece of information.

The answer was hidden, but plain as day, screaming out to the deaf ears of the FBI profiler and MSNBC news reporter. Manson's mother, according to the narrator, was a seventeen-year-old heavy drinker working the streets. Once, she tried to sell her baby for a pitcher of beer. Absolutely no link was made to her drinking while she was pregnant and the resulting brain damage inflicted on her child. Yes, he is a killer, but the simple truth is, he has brain damage caused by prenatal exposure to alcohol and is not some mystical, romanticized Hannibal Lector.

In the case of the Omaha Mall shooter, mentioned at the outset of this chapter, the Omaha Press, in a single sentence at the end of an article written days later, stated his long-gone biological mother was a binge drinker. Once again, no link was drawn between his actions and his mother's drinking.

In 1966, my hometown of Grand Rapids, MN, experienced the first school shooting in the nation, in which a school administrator, Forrest L. Willey, was killed by a student who brought a gun to school to shoot another student. In 2005, Jeff Weise became the most prolific single shooter in the nation at the Red Lake High School in Minnesota. I was uniquely positioned to see the connection to prenatal exposure to alcohol. In 2008, I completed my research into the connection between school shooters and their mother's drinking habits. My research revealed when enough information could be found, 82 percent of school shooters, including the most prolific shootings of Columbine and Red Lake, fit the profile of prenatal exposure to alcohol. Mothers and close relatives of mothers were interviewed and confirmed the exposure. My book, *The Fatal Link*, (Outskirts Press, 2008) revealed for the first time this connection.

The only way to start to stem the tide is to understand the depth of the problem. We need to start asking the question every time a violent or deviant act takes place, every time a student is assigned a Special Education Individual Education Plan, every time a mother gives birth, every time a child is medicated for behavioral reasons, every time a criminal is tried in court, every time an inmate is incarcerated, every time a person becomes a client in the social system. Only then will we know how much a mother exposing her fetus to alcohol impacts us all. Only then will we truly know the root cause of America's Greatest Brain Drain.

That is some amazing research that Jody has put together. I encourage you to buy his book, *The Fatal Link,* and learn more about this root issue in America. Please allow me to make some observations about what we just heard before we move on to the next chapter.

1. We can be born with a predisposition but not conceived with that same predisposition.

2. Like fatherless homes in the previous chapter, prenatal exposure to alcohol not only affects crime as the "fatal link" but also impacts many other major social concerns of our day.

3. This type of information has to get out to the public fast. As deadly as secondhand smoke is to our society, so we see the same for second-hand drinking.

The last three chapters and respective case studies have dealt with social issues and their root causes. While this is still fresh in our minds, let's summarize these chapters. I think you will find this interesting.

CASE STUDY	SURFACE ISSUE	A ROOT ISSUE
#1	Obesity Emotional Eating (Having a Relationship with Food)	Child Abuse
#2	Crime Lower Graduation Rates Welfare	Time and Trauma in Children
#3	Crime Mental Disorders/Increased Medications Achievement Gaps	Prenatal Exposure to Alcohol

What do you see as you analyze this table? As I look at this table, it appears that a strong case can be made for the idea that we are destroying ourselves. The specific vehicle for that destruction is dysfunctional family structures. Nations can survive a lot of calamity and strife, but a stable and functional family structure is essential for survival. Japan has survived a high amount of debt, but they only have a 2 percent out-of-wed-lock birthrate. Iraq has survived thirty years of wars, I believe in large part, because they still have a strong family and tribal system. We will touch on these internal threats more in chapter seven. As we walk away from these chapters on social issues, I hope you will agree with me that we have a root reality here that we need to get our minds around.

I hope the opening two chapters along with the three case studies that followed demonstrates to you the need to go beyond the thirty second sound bites on the news. I hope you can see how much the diagnosis changes after including the root issues in the examination. Now that we have established and validated this method of examination, let's apply the same method to our nation's government.

Starting in the next chapter, we will transition to politics and leadership. Later, in chapters nine and ten, we will bring together three proposed root solutions.

ROOT LESSON FROM CHAPTER FIVE:

The behavior of one generation can permanently alter the next generation.

6

A ROOT CAUSE OF THE NATIONAL DEBT

A glazed look came over my wife's face. Jeanne had a tremendous capacity to listen to less-than-interesting stories about my day at work. But hearing long explanations about budgets and deficits really pushed the marital bliss to the edge. Jeanne does, however, enjoy hearing about anything that invokes humility in her husband, especially when it comes to farm animals. I have worked with hundreds of farmers over fifteen years as an employee with a major corporation. The last twelve years, I helped farmers with their overall management techniques. In other words, I was a business consultant. My wife especially likes the story in which I was talking to a farmer in Minnesota about his chicken feed (yes, chicken feed) and while we were wrapping up the conversation, a hen landed right on top of my head and sat down. I was so surprised and embarrassed I did not reference the hen on my head for a couple of minutes. The farmer went on engaging in the conversation as if this kind of thing happened to everyone who stopped by his farm.

Who can talk about farm animals without talking about the farm dog? We all know the farm dog is the first farm animal to greet you upon your arrival. I have been bitten by dogs, my tires have been bitten by dogs, and my leg has been peed on by dogs. Once you have been bitten and peed on, you have endured the worst, and it should get better from there. Cats can be the funniest. One day a cat ran up my back unannounced at full speed only to stop and rest on the top of my head. The cat stayed long enough for the embarrassed farm wife to reach up and take the cat into her own arms and give her pet some attention. I think the farm wife demonstrated more hospitality than the man who left the hen just sitting on my head. My point here is that I know where to go when I need a dose of humility and how to redirect the conversation with my wife when budgets get boring. Farm pets generally provide humor and life to any rural setting and even to those just visiting.

But on the opposite end of the spectrum is something called debt. It has the ability to provide sorrow and death to a business. Once in a great while, I was assigned a farm business that was struggling with debt. The degree of debt at times was to the point of risking the well-being of the business. I will describe a specific example in the next chapter. These were difficult situations, to say the least. The families were always the nicest people you could meet. In the end you could refinance, restructure, make recommendations, agree on new ideas, and refinance again, but often the managers either didn't have the natural ability to implement the needed changes or the capacity to change their behavior.

I have seen what debt can do to a business, both good and bad. Debt can cause jobs to be created, and debt can cause jobs to go away. There is a fine line between managing debt and debt managing you. The housing industry stepped over the line too many times, and now we

132 | STEVEN J. WILSON

have homes upside down in debt across the nation. Every industry generally has a benchmark of acceptable debt. In the housing market, an acceptable debt might be 85 percent debt. Low-risk businesses might be 75 percent debt. Higher-risk businesses might be 65 percent debt. However, 50 percent debt is usually a safe number for most endeavors.

When it comes to the federal debt, the numbers are actually not much different; however, the unit of measurement is completely different. Private business will measure debt as a percent of assets. The national debt is measured as a percent of the GDP or Gross Domestic Product of the nation. This unit of measurement (percent of GDP) allows economists and citizens to compare debt across history on an apples-to-apples comparison. You can see the changes in our nation's debt since the early 1900s in this chart compiled by the Concord Coalition.

HISTORY OF U.S. NATIONAL DEBT

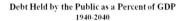

Debt Held by the Public as a Percent of GDP
1940-2040

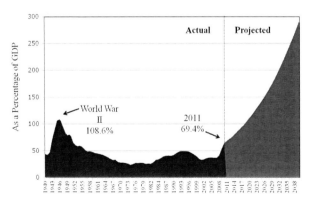

Source: GAO Analysis, Feb. 2011 and OMB Historical Tables 2011 and compiled by Concord Coalition.

Why all the fuss about the rising national debt? Take a look at the future in the federal debt chart. Many experts would say 50 to 60 percent (debt held by the public as a percent of GDP) is just fine. However, as we approach 90 percent, economies can slow down, and as we reach 100 percent, the alarms should be going off. This is generally unsustainable territory, especially if you have borrowed a lot of money from other countries rather than your own citizens. That is one of the big differences between Japan's debt and the U.S. debt. Much of Japan's debt is borrowed from their own citizens. Not so with the United States. Roughly half of the U.S. public debt is now borrowed from foreign lenders. In fact, the United States has borrowed roughly one trillion dollars from China alone.

CHINA

I heard a main street business owner say that if the national debt gets too much higher, we'd better start learning Chinese! This generally creates a nervous laugh from people. So, what about China? A few years ago, I was serving on the government affairs committee of our local chamber of commerce. We were invited to listen to a guest speaker who was a Chinese businessman with a branch here in the United States. I was struck by his boldness. He made sure to point out that in a matter of time, China's economy would be larger than the U.S. economy. He had charts showing us the specific year it was projected to happen. I could understand his number, but I struggled in sharing his enthusiasm for America coming in second place. His information certainly demonstrates that China has been studying the United States.

It seems Americans need to learn a bit more about China. The Chinese have a real interest in both our nation's public and private sectors. In addition to owning a trillion dollars of our public debt,[48] they are continuing to buy our private sector. The Chinese invested $1.73 billion in U.S. projects and acquisitions in 2009 according to a Bloomberg *Businessweek* article. Just through the first nine months of 2010, the same investments were $2.81 billion.[49] Many would say this is good since they are bringing jobs to the United States. That may be true, but on the return trip they bring our technology back to their own factories in China, not to mention that America owns less and less of America. The United States may have some short-term benefits; however, the long-term benefits are less compelling.

As we move through this chapter, I want to be careful because I know numbers can drown a person quickly. I promise you I am going to take a different route than you would generally see when the national debt is discussed. I am going to take the "root route," if you will. If you are interested in the details of surface issues such as the Social Security Trust Fund, distinguishing between debt held by the public and gross debt, the Medicare Trust Fund or debt held by foreign investors, I would suggest reading *Come Back America* by David M. Walker. He is the former head of the Government Accountability Office. If you want a historical perspective, you may want to follow the writings of Harvard historian Niall Ferguson. The book you are reading now will focus on root issues and the paradigm shift needed to address these issues. Allow me to give just a bit more background, and then I will move in that direction.

With a twenty-year background in working with private business debt, I was fascinated to study the nation's public debt. In the economic world, this is called switching from *microeconomics* to *macroeconomics*. I enjoy them both. In the last few years, I have been a guest speaker at several colleges as well as civic and political venues discussing the direction of our nation as it relates to borrowing money. I am a grassroots activist when it comes to the national debt. Part of what brought me up to speed quickly was a mentor. I owe a debt of gratitude to a man in our city by the name of Bill Plummer. Bill spent hours with me at his kitchen table, on the phone, through e-mail and in the car teaching me about Social Security, Medicare, and the national debt. Thanks to Bill and a lot of national resources, I will draw some comparisons from microeconomics and private debt to macroeconomics and our national public debt.

LEADERSHIP

To set the stage, I will give you all sides of the story regarding attempts to solve the national debt from early 2010 to early 2011. First of all, President Obama showed great leadership by issuing an executive order to establish the fiscal debt commission, formally known as the *National Commission on Fiscal Responsibility and Reform.* Just a few weeks before his announcement during the State of the Union address, a measure to deal with the national debt called the Conrad Judd Act had failed to pass the Senate. Take note: the Senate was the responsible party in this situation. After the failure in the Senate, there was nothing in play to address this crucial issue. The president's leadership was needed, and he provided it. The debt commission was put in place and was successful in assembling a bold set of recommendations. The report was issued in December of 2010. The commission failed to achieve the necessary fourteen of eighteen votes because the House Republicans for some unknown reason all voted "no" on the recommendations. This was sad because even though it was not binding, it was a consensus for a resolution. Take note, the House was the responsible party in this situation.

Next the Ryan plan was introduced from the House Budget Committee and was a bold plan as well, with the size and scope needed to attack the monstrous debt. President Obama presented his own plan in April of 2011. Instead of setting politics aside, the president blasted the Ryan plan rather than finding a way to work with the Ryan plan. Take note, the president was the responsible party in this situation.

As you can see, leadership from all sides has struggled to get on the same page. This is where the light finally went on in my mind. I have seen this before. There is something else going on here. Whenever I experienced the unwillingness of others to properly manage rising debt with small business, it usually was not a surface issue. It was almost always a root issue. Something was going on under the surface issue that was causing the problem. With private business, we would treat the symptoms (surface issues), and the problem would come back. In the situation of the federal debt, even the surface issue was not changing.

This unwillingness to properly manage the national debt has been going on for decades in our nation. Therefore, let's not get caught on a rabbit trail of one party or the other. This is something that is beyond the party issue. Party politics is a surface issue. The fact this issue has been going on for so long demonstrates strong evidence of a root issue. There is a cultural root issue in politics, and we the citizens are the only ones who can accept the blame. There is something very strong under the surface, and we have to get to the bottom of it. We have to find the root of the problem.

This is the point in the chapter where I am going to switch directions. I would like to suggest to you that our national debt is not just a budget issue alone. There is also a bigger root issue to deal with. I believe the root issue is a behavioral issue. In my experience with small businesses, many times the problem was not the budget but one of two other issues: either a lack of natural ability to manage debt or a behavioral issue. Both natural ability and behavior were root issues, not surface issues.

Before we dig into the root issue and give you specifics, let's stop and think about chapter one and remind ourselves why root discoveries are vital. There are two important reasons. First, if there is a root issue, it completely changes the solution. Second, if the surface issue is fixed but not the root issue, the problem will pop back up again down the road, perhaps at a time even less convenient.

Now let's dig deeper. First of all, what specific behavior could this root issue be? I will be bold here and say that it is an issue of being inwardly focused rather than being outwardly focused. That's it. The root problem is a political culture that is inwardly focused. This is clear to see when we look at the list of priorities of nearly every political incumbent and even of most challengers. His or her priority list might look like this:

1. My reelection or election

2. My party

3. My special interest groups

4. The voters I represent

5. The nation

What do we see when we look closer? The first three items of the list are inward in nature. Not until we reach priority four do we see a true outward focus. So, this is it. This is the root issue we must deal with as a nation. We are dealing with a political culture that is inwardly focused. This issue is as important if not more important than dealing with the surface issue. Now we have lots to talk about.

Many of you will look at this list and say, "Okay, but this has been a problem for awhile. Why is this any more of a problem today?" It is normal for a lot of root issues to be underestimated or passed over until the situation is under tremendous pressure. A garden hose may have a tiny leak but will not be noticed until it is under pressure. A fire engine that does not start is not a big problem until there is a fire. A small business may not realize there is a problem root issue until it is under financial pressure. I have seen this dozens of times. In the case of our nation, good economic conditions can provide tremendous cover for a growing root issue. Now that the pressure of the debt is mounting, it is easier to see the root issue. This is the case with our federal government. This inward-focused culture is tolerated as long as the money is flowing and the debt is manageable. But now that the economy has been slower and the debt is rising quickly, we have pressure.

Is there any data to support this political priority list? A recent poll by the Center on Congress at Indiana University asked the question, "What do you think is the main thing that influences what members of Congress do in office?" Eighty-four percent of those surveyed believe that either *personal interest* or *special interests* drive congressional action.[50] The root problem is obvious. The inwardly focused culture has to be dealt with. Let's look at some concerns when we have a list of priorities that are inwardly focused.

HARMONY AND CONFLICT

The five items on the list are absolutely problematic. Sometimes all five are in harmony, and sometimes they are in direct conflict with each other. The national debt just happens to be one of those items that force priority-one and priority-five to be in direct conflict. There is little to reconcile between these two priorities when it comes to the topic of the national debt.

SPECIAL INTEREST GROUPS

One example of a loss of self-control is reelection campaigns funded by special interest groups. Would you believe there are campaigns in which nearly 90 percent of the campaign dollars are donated by special interest groups? Yes, 90 percent. If you would like to do some research for yourself, it is public information at www.fec.gov. So, who is that representative representing? One could argue the voters from that district have a representative in name alone. If you look closely at the FEC websites, you will see many if not most U.S. Representatives get the majority of their money from a combination of special interest groups and money from donors outside their district.

PUBLIC SERVANT

The top three priorities were not part of the original intent of the job. The whole nature of the job was to serve others (the public), in other words, to be outwardly focused. Many members of Congress have lost their self-control in these areas. Even freshman congressmen and women who have a mandate to reduce the debt were dancing around tough questions three months after the 2010 election because they have already seemingly committed to priority one.

INCUMBENTS RULE

Another reason Congress can get away with this inwardly focused approach is because incumbents statistically have a 90-plus percent chance of being reelected. Spinning this around, if any member of Congress can risk being outwardly focused, it should be the incumbents. They should be the ones demonstrating an outwardly focused mindset to the newer members.

PRE-SCREENED CANDIDATES

What solidifies this priority list is the prescreening of new candidates. Unless you happen to be a person who fits into the mold of this priority list, new candidates may have little success in getting endorsed, let alone elected. You see, we citizens at the grassroots level are responsible too.

CITIZENS

I have beaten up on the federal government long enough, so now let me turn to you and me. The second root issue under our national debt has to do with the voter and our individual ability to sacrifice. Are you and I willing to give something up to help our nation? Are we committed to shared sacrifice, or are we committed to someone else's shared sacrifice? We the voters have to examine our ability to be outwardly focused as well. Here we have another root issue that will require self-discipline to manage. Shared sacrifice is the only equitable approach that we have to consider. What are you and I willing to give up for the interest of the common good or in this case the future of our nation? We have gradually become addicted to the goodies that our elected representatives have dangled in front of us to help position themselves for re-election, goodies that may not even really go directly through the legislative process. I hope we may never forget President Kennedy's famous statement, "Ask not what your country can do for you—ask what you can do for your country." Let's remember, this challenge was made before Medicare even existed.

Now that we have identified two root issues, let's imagine what it could look like if these two root issues went away. Let's start with the root issue of a political culture that is inwardly focused. What if we could find a way to change to an outwardly focused political culture?

MEDICARE

Medicare is the toughest surface issue of our day to talk about. It is easy to fix but hard to talk about. Why? If you give an honest answer, you will not be reelected. Seniors and soon-to-be seniors vote in high percentages, and they will not be excited about a change in Medicare. However, left untouched, Medicare has the potential to single-handedly take down this nation at some point in the future. It is very hard to find a leader who will give a direct answer. It is generally smoothed off around the edges. Let me give you an answer with one item changed. Priority number five on the list, the nation, becomes priority one, and the others move down. I have now become outwardly focused.

Before I make a general statement about Medicare, I want to clarify that I realize there are four parts of Medicare; each of the four will more or less hold true to my general statement. Now, let me summarize Medicare in one sentence from a mathematical perspective. Generally speaking, *Medicare is a finite number of dollars coming into a pool with an infinite number of dollars going out of the same pool in the form of benefits.*

Until you change the formula, the problem will not go away. The formula needs to change to this: *Medicare is a finite number of dollars coming into a pool with a finite number of dollars going out of the same pool in the form of benefits.* What does that mean in practical terms? At some point in the future, Medicare will need to be reformed with some benefits limited. Every person enrolled in Medicare will have access to some amount of benefits, and any remaining benefits will have to come from someplace outside of Medicare. We may all have dreams of having the nicest car or the biggest house, but in the end it comes down to numbers. We cannot keep buying the new car and house if we do not have the income to support the purchases. It is not sound government leadership to keep spending more in Medicare than is being taken in.

This hot subject is easy for me to talk about because I simply moved number five to the top of the priority list. I am less concerned with my reelection, less concerned with my party, and less concerned with my special interest groups. My top interest is what is best for the nation. Once the root issue changes, the surface issue changes easily. The main thing that is holding us back from fixing Medicare tomorrow is being inwardly focused today.

In chapter nine I will provide a solution that addresses the root issue of a political culture that is inwardly focused. This alone will not get the job done. The other root issue is a citizenry that is unwilling to sacrifice. As we saw in the mathematical formula above, Medicare has to fundamentally change, or the problem will not go away. That means sacrifice. Medicare is only one example. We will need shared sacrifice across the nation.

THE RIGHT CAUSE WILL
MOTIVATE PEOPLE TO SACRIFICE

So, why are we Americans unwilling to sacrifice? Why are we unwilling to work through this second root issue? Here is my opinion. Medicare is only the surface issue. In the next couple of paragraphs, I am going make some bold statements. The root cause we are fighting for in this nation is actually sovereignty. If the citizens of this great nation had a sense they were fighting for our sovereignty, the enthusiasm to sacrifice would be different. What I am saying here is that if our nation goes bankrupt, Medicare will be of little concern compared to our sovereignty. In other words, whether or not we have the freedom to make our own choices as a nation should be the front and center issue.

When will we see our sovereignty diminished or compromised? Now I am going to get even bolder. Our sovereignty is being compromised right now. In 2009, something happened that only received token-news attention. It may only be symbolic or it may have long-term consequences. At one point in late summer 2009, our nation crossed the 50 percent mark of public debt held by foreigners. In other words, less than 50 percent of our public debt was held by Americans. Now to be fair, in an annual report issued by the U.S. Treasury Department in June of 2011, the number was back under 50 percent.[51] And to provide the full picture, the debt held by foreign lenders was 32.0 percent of the gross or total debt. How does this 32.0 percent compare with the past? This same number in 1994, for example, was 14.8 percent. Is this change in borrowing from foreigners bad? This change by itself is not terrible. It is the ramifications that can be troubling, especially as it relates to our sovereignty.

Let me give you a scenario that might demonstrate what I am talking about. We know North Korea has been testing missiles. What if North Korea assembled a long-range missile with a nuclear warhead that was pointed at Alaska? In other words, we have a looming national threat. What would be the response from the United States, and, specifically, what would our conversation look like with China? Would we *declare* our intentions to defend our land or would we *discuss* our intentions to defend our land? Keep in mind, any attempt to defend our nation that would cause China to be upset would risk our ability to sell all those U.S. Treasury bonds to China. Without China buying our Treasury bonds, the demand for bonds decreases and the interest rate we pay increases. In the end our nation is not only encumbered with the military cost to defend our nation, we may likely also encumber a higher interest expense on our national debt. The decision-making process gets more and more complicated.

The question that comes to mind as I think about this level of foreign debt is this: are we still a nation with 100 percent sovereignty? Are we at 99 percent sovereignty? Are we at 93 percent sovereignty? If you have ever taken out a loan on a building, you know that if you want to make any major changes to that building, you need the permission of the lender or, at least, have a discussion with them. Even if your basic financial situation changes to any great degree, the bank wants to know. In this situation, you do not have 100 percent sovereignty over your decision. You are obligated to have a discussion with the lender.

It is the same with our lender, China. I believe we are already having discussions with China, assuring them of our ability to pay our debts. Therefore, I believe our sovereignty is already less than 100 percent. It comes with the territory. I think we have entered into the entry-level stages of being a slave to our lenders. It may only be one toe in the water, but it is happening. How long will it take before we grow comfortable with something less than 100 percent sovereignty? How long until this compromise of our sovereignty become a habit and then a behavior? How long before our behavior starts to drive our core values? In other words, our addiction to debt is stronger than the core value of sovereignty.

Again, Medicare is not the root cause. It is a surface item. I believe sovereignty is the root cause we need to be fighting for in this nation. Instead of carrying a sign saying, "Hands off my Medicare," it should say, "Hands off my Sovereignty." Since the priority list of our political leaders is inwardly focused, few will be willing to admit that our nation is fighting for sovereignty. Such a statement would invite cries of, "The sky is falling!" and would decrease the chances for reelection. Without this clear understanding of what we are potentially risking, the nation lacks any real sense of need to sacrifice and therefore any real reason to sacrifice.

Even if you are not convinced that our sovereignty is already being compromised, let me point out to you how quickly it can be lost. Many of you who have taken out a loan on a house are familiar with fixed rate versus variable interest rates. Perhaps the term "ARM" or Adjustable Rate Mortgage is something you have toyed with during the financing process. The problem with an ARM is risk. If rates go up all of a sudden, your mortgage liability and obligation can increase dramatically. What many people do not realize is that much of our existing federal debt is similar to an ARM. Much of our old federal debt is refinanced every year. And if you look closer at the tables from the U.S. Treasury, you will see that at any given time, the United States will generally need to refinance 70 percent of its old debt in the next five years. That means if people stopped lending to the United States, we could lose our ability to function quickly and potentially lose our sovereignty with it. Since we are borrowing money to make our principal and interest payments, it could all happen in a very short period of time.

So, let's take this for a test run. What happens if we have changed the cause we are fighting for to *sovereignty* and away from *Medicare*?

Let me give you a very simple outcome or solution if we make this one adjustment. A possible resolution could be a Sovereignty Protection Act. This SPA would simply state that a given year's growth in the GDP would be the next year's rise in the debt ceiling. For example, if the GDP rose by a trillion dollars one year, the national debt ceiling could only raise by one trillion the next year. From a practical application perspective, I would initially add two caveats. One is that there should be a two-year lag for planning purposes. In other words, the economy or GDP grows by a trillion in 2012. The debt ceiling would increase by a trillion in 2014. The second caveat is to use this as a safety net. This second mechanism would provide the sovereignty preservation element. It would look like this: the measure would only be activated when the gross or total debt to GDP ratio reached 110 percent. Obviously this mechanism would generally keep the gross debt to GDP around 110 percent both in the short and long term. Hopefully we would have the self-discipline to bring the ratio back down to 50 percent at some time in the future.

An even simpler version is to use the debt held by the public as a share of GDP along with a safety net of 100 percent. If the public debt as a share of GDP was approaching 100 percent in 2018, for example, then the actual amount of GDP in 2018 would determine the public debt ceiling for 2020. In other words, if the GDP in 2018 was 16 trillion, then the debt ceiling for the debt held by the public for 2020 would be 16 trillion. This would assure that the public debt to GDP would always stay below 100 percent so long as the economy was growing.

This would be an example of an SPA that the average American could easily understand. Secondly, as you look at the federal debt chart in this chapter, you can see there is a clear historical precedent. A lot more detail and planning would need to go into the Sovereignty Protection Act, but you get the picture.

PEP TALK!

At this point, "we the people" have to consider the long-term sustainability of this nation. I ask you today, "Do we really love our country, or do we just love the prosperity?" Are we going to be the generation that sucks the life out of an empire and then leave? We are in need of grassroots action by patriots who have an attitude of selfless service to a great nation. We have lived in the most prosperous generation since the beginning of the world. Wouldn't that seem to be enough? Giving up some Medicare benefits should be small potatoes in the grand scheme of a great nation. With this perspective, a compromise can be found so another generation can see this nation as it was meant to be. Personally, I am not opposed to raising some revenues as a form of compromise to reform Medicare, but the mathematical formula still has to be fundamentally changed *first*, as we indicated at the beginning of our discussion on Medicare.

So, changing the surface issue is easy. Simply change the formula. The real issue is the two root issues of behavior. Both the federal government and the voter need to become outwardly focused.

HISTORICAL VIEW

As you know, our nation has a history of outwardly focused leaders and citizenry that sacrificed repeatedly for the good of the nation. Take a look at the last time the national debt was over 100 percent as a share of the GDP. As you can see on the debt chart, it was in 1944. Compare the difference on the chart between now and then. In 1944, we as a nation quickly cut the debt in half.

This time we will quickly double it. Why? Some would say we were not dealing with the rising cost of Medicare in the 1940s. True. But I think that is closer to a surface issue than a root issue. Both now and then, we are and were coming out of war time. So, we can't blame it on that. I believe we had a different nation at that time. From 1929 until the late 1940s, self-sacrifice was part of who we were. We had come through the Great Depression and then WWII. Hopefully, we have all met people who have grown up during the Depression. That generation had self-discipline like no other. They also had tremendous ability to *go without* and use self-sacrifice. Ironically our society was more outwardly focused when we had less in our pockets. The sacrificial approach in the 1940s and 1950s resulted in physically paying down debt rather than setting new borrowing records as we see today.

Let's go back even further in time. What about Abraham Lincoln? What do you think his priorities looked like? Did President Lincoln avoid the Emancipation Proclamation because it would jeopardize his reelection? No. Did he avoid the Emancipation Proclamation because his political party would suffer in the next election? No. Did he avoid the Emancipation Proclamation because it might affect funding dollars from his special interest groups? Hardly.

Here is what President Lincoln had to say about his reelection chances: "I am going to be beaten," he told an army officer, "and unless some great change takes place, badly beaten."[52] In regard to fallout from his own Republican Party, the Democratic Party did indeed make gains in the congressional elections of

November 1862. It did not stop there. Some of his own party supported John C. Fremont for the Republican nomination instead of Lincoln. President Lincoln was undoubtedly outwardly focused and took risk to be outwardly focused. This is leadership. He was less concerned with reelection, his newly founded party, or other risks of the day. His first priority was the nation and its long-term future "that this nation, under God, shall have a new birth of freedom and that government of the people, by the people, for the people, shall not perish from the earth."[53]

What about George Washington? Do you think he was worried about his possible campaign for president, possible political party, and possible special interest money during the Revolutionary War? Hardly. It is a historical fact that he just wanted to go back to his farm. From a historical perspective, being outwardly focused is part of the character of the political leaders when our nation was under pressure.

STRATEGY

So, let's assume we have changed the political culture from inwardly focused to outwardly focused and changed the cause we are all fighting for from Medicare to Sovereignty. There is still one more strategic item that is necessary in order to change the national debt. It is in the area of chronological order.

When I first came home from Iraq in 2009, my mentor, Bill Plummer, and I were giving grassroots-level speeches about the national debt. During these talks we stressed a very important factor. Before making any decision on Medicare or Social Security reform (surface issues), a framework would need to be agreed upon by Congress. An example of that framework is the SPA I, briefly outlined above. Again, the specific strategic element is the chronological order of the SPA. If we try to pass Medicare or Social Security reforms before a framework is fully structured, we could risk losing all the momentum and quickly suffer a crash in negotiation of a plan to solve the national debt. The framework has to come first. I describe this more in chapter nine.

We stressed this concern in 2009, and I still feel strongly about this today. If we dabble in reform first or at the same time, it will be too tempting for the inwardly focused political culture to flare up and hold these reforms against the other party for the purpose of making political hay. Once we get the framework or SPA in place, we can have the reform discussion on surface issues. At that point we will for sure need an outwardly focused Congress to make the reforms needed. The reforms even after the framework is in place may likely result in several one-term congressmen and women. However, the outwardly focused self-sacrifice will allow a nation that prospers into the future.

In the last few chapters, we have identified at least five root issues in our nation. Three of those were social root issues and were summarized at the end of chapter five. In this chapter we identified two political root issues: political leaders who are inwardly focused and citizens who are unsure about sacrifice. We will use these root issues to make a better diagnosis in the next chapter and then look for specific solutions in chapter nine.

CHAPTER 6

ROOT LESSON FROM CHAPTER SIX:

Prevent all behavior that allows
slavery to debt.

7

A BETTER DIAGNOSIS FOR OUR NATION

They were the nicest farm family you would ever want to meet. They had all the pieces in place for being a successful business, that is, except for one. Yes, they had great core values and were disciplined in their work habits and behavior, but they did not have the natural ability to manage debt. Their debt was managing them. It was sad because it was easy to really like this family. As a business consultant, I was asked to help them work with their banker. I felt like a doctor who was asked to help a stage-three or stage-four cancer patient. You can rerun the tests, or in this case rerun the cash flows and refinance the debt, but it will yield little difference in the outcome. Eventually, the farm was sold, and the family moved. Today if you drive by the farm, there are no remnants of a busy farm operation. No longer is there a line of silos that stand up across the horizon as the sun is setting. There is no lingering smell of fresh green hay in the air. The new owners eliminated the buildings and developed the land. Today if you drive by the former farming operation, you will only see new homes that have parceled up the land with new owners who have no knowledge of the farm that occupied that same land just a few years earlier. The new owners have little interest in the former owner and could not even care less.

This is one story of a misdiagnosed business. It appeared from a distance that all was well. However, no one took the time to diagnose the root issues of the business. And when it was discovered that there was indeed a root issue underneath the surface, it was too late to make the necessary changes. Time ran out, and the business went away. If only there would have been a better diagnosis.

This can happen with nations and empires, too. It has happened. My main reason for writing this book is because I love our country, and I believe we have a short amount of time to change course. It is a crucial time to properly diagnose this nation. There are a lot of good people making great speeches and sound bites but not taking the time to check their assumptions and ask about root issues. I am fearful that we will not fully consider the root issues. And if we do consider them, will it be too late? I think as we have demonstrated in our examples that there is a better diagnosis. In obesity, it is not always about the diet or the food. It is often about satisfying a need for comfort. It is not a surface issue; it is a root issue. With crime, it is less about policy or law. It is about time and trauma. It is not a surface issue; it is a root issue. As we dug deeper in chapter five, it was less about medicating mental disorders and more about prenatal exposure to alcohol. It is not a surface issue. It is a root issue. With the nation's debt, it is not just about budgets. It is about leaders being inwardly focused and citizens unsure about shared sacrifice. It is not a surface issue alone; there are root issues too. A better diagnosis for our nation is to acknowledge the threat of root and surface issues, not just surface issues alone.

PRUNING THE PROBLEM

Our current political approach in handling social issues is not working. In chapter two I introduced an example. Here is the full explanation and wouldn't you know, it starts in the garden. If we prune a weed, the surface looks better and may actually be better in the short term, but the root is still there. The weed comes back. The same is true in the social and political realm. In this book, I call it "pruning the problem." When we only consider the surface issues, this is what happens. We see our children struggling with issues such as nutrition, achievement gaps, and access to health care. What do we do? We only attack the surface. We respond with government programs for more free lunches in our schools, and we all feel better that something is being done. A few years later, the root issue has not been addressed and the surface issue comes back, so we expand the government funding for the program. Next, we add more early education programs, and we all feel better that something is being done. A few years later, the root issue has not been addressed and the surface issue comes back, so we expand the government funding for the program. Next, we expand health care for children and feel better that something is being done. A few years later, the root issue has not been addressed and the surface issue comes back, so we expand the government funding for the program.

Do you see what is happening? The only result is a short-term fix and a few short-term political votes for those adding the programs. The real problem is the root issue is still there. Functional fathers are still not reporting for duty as leaders and providers with the mothers. The father is absent without leave. He is still not helping to provide the lunch the child needs. He is still not sitting down to read with his child at night. He is still not helping to provide for the emotional and physical health of the child. As a matter of fact, as we have seen earlier in the book, the rate of fatherless homes has doubled. Out-of-wedlock birthrates have skyrocketed to 40 percent in our nation.[54]

The short-term social benefits provide cover for the root issue to multiply. Socially there has been some short-term benefit to individual children, but as a society, we have not made the strides needed. Political individuals tout their achievements and garner some votes as we move further behind as a nation. So we march on and continue to treat the symptoms rather than the true cause. We continue to call ourselves gardeners, yet our credentials only lie in our ability to prune the problem.

One of the potent risks in discussing pruning the problem is when it is mixed with an inwardly focused Congress. The temptation is huge to use this as fodder for discrediting an opponent rather than allowing the issue to be put on the table. The idea is quickly and easily spun to sound like we are anti-children. In reality the ultimate goal is a mom and dad sitting on the couch at night with their young children in their laps and reading a book together. That is my interest. That is my vision of what is at the core of a functional society and is part of a healthy nation. The government is the direct benefactor of this approach. However, it is hard to fit this in a ten-second sound bite, so the spinning wins and discredits the thought before the full story is told.

In this chapter we will look at the collective effect of these mounting root issues and what it means for the future of our nation. As I have demonstrated in this book, obesity, fatherless homes, and the national debt have doubled in the last twenty-five years. As we study these three generally unrelated areas of our nation, we come across something that compels us to ask even more questions. If the trend line of the last five years is extrapolated out further, we find that it is possible for all three of these to double again. Specifically, extrapolating the most recent data from the last five years forward for the national debt and fatherless homes leaves us doubling these two again in twenty years. If we do the same for obesity, it will double again in thirty years.

Here is my takeaway from looking at this information. As we look at the future of our nation, the biggest threat to our well-being will no longer be external threats. Our biggest threat to our well-being will be our internal threats. Clearly, we will still have external threats, but the internal threats have the ability to bring this nation to its social and financial knees. What can happen next, as we have seen in other crumbling empires, is the inability to uphold a strong military. As in the story I used to open this chapter, our nation does not want to have the same ending.

Now it becomes obvious we have to ask more questions. It is imperative we study the risk of internal threats.

WHAT DO THESE INTERNAL THREATS COST?

If I only consider the three internal threats I have identified in the previous chapters, the current estimated cost for these internal threats is over $500 billion per year. Obesity, according to the CDC, is $75 billion.[55] I estimated in chapter four that the cost of fatherless homes is over $224 billion, and interest on the national debt is budgeted at $242 billion for fiscal year 2012.[56] The three together brings us to $541 billion. Let's get some perspective on this. The current cost of our military to manage the external threats is $884 billion[57] per year, and as mentioned, the estimated cost to manage our internal threats is over $500 billion per year. We could survive just fine if the current costs stayed the same.

Here is the problem. This scenario will very likely reverse itself within ten years. This should cause the alarms to go off as we consider our future. The projected budget for our military in 2021 is $914 billion,[58] and the cost to manage our internal threats will be between one and two trillion. As a matter of fact, according to the Government Accountability Office's (GAO) alternative model, interest on the debt alone will be hovering around a trillion a year.[59] The fact that these two numbers are projected to reverse is likely a first in our nation's history. Certainly this is an indicator of a pending financial implosion. Remember, as we consider the cost of internal threats, we have not even touched on home-grown terrorists, the rising cost of health care, or any other potential internal threats.

If internal threats could bring this nation to a cliff in the next ten years and if root issues lie underneath the surface issues, then we should be better able to properly diagnose our nation. A better diagnosis for our nation is to acknowledge the threat of root and surface issues, not just surface issues alone. We need to solve the surface issues and the root issues both. We can no longer minimize or ignore the root issues in our nation.

We discussed projections of ten years into the future. What will our nation become in twenty years if trends in obesity, fatherless homes and the national debt continue? According to the GAO alternative simulation in 2012, the federal government may only have enough resources to pay interest on the debt, social security, and some medicare and medicaid in twenty years if current trends continue. In other words, no defense or any other discretionary dollars would be made available to the federal government. Add the obesity and fatherless homes to the equation and the result is a nation that will struggle to exist as we know it today.

A better diagnosis is to admit we have a cultural issue at the root level.

These are the very things our Founding Fathers warned us about. For example, when George Washington had finished his eight years as president, he delivered one of the most important speeches in American history. He delivered a farewell speech in 1797. In the middle of that wise speech, he made the statement, "Of all the dispositions and habits which lead to political prosperity, religion and morality are indispensable supports. In vain would that man claim the tribute of patriotism who should labor to subvert these great pillars of human happiness."[60] The father of our nation was concerned about cultural issues at the root level. He was especially concerned about core values.

CORE VALUES

The founders were wonderful at keeping written documents of their work. Some of the words during the founding era reference core values. Some of those values are virtue, respect, morality, self-discipline, honor, duty, humility, and sacrifice. This is what we mean when we say positive core values. The founders assumed the people to be inwardly sound.

If I were to assess our root issues as a whole in this nation, I would have to say we have an increasing lack of self-control. The antidote is a core value called self-discipline. It actually ties core values and behavior together. We should not confuse self-control with self-discipline. Self-control is the result of self-discipline. If we want more self-control, we need to increase self-discipline. Nor should we confuse personal responsibility with self-discipline. Personal responsibility only points to who is responsible. If we want to ask what we are responsible for, one answer is self-discipline.

SELF-DISCIPLINE

If we have root issues that need attention, we will look to root solutions. Chapters nine and ten will deal with those specifically. The remainder of this chapter and the next chapter will set the stage for those solutions. I would encourage you not to skip ahead. The solutions chapter will make more sense to you with the foundation I am about to establish. After looking closer at obesity, fatherless homes, and the national debt, it would seem that self-discipline would be a personal characteristic to dig into. *Webster* defines discipline as this: "Training that corrects, molds or perfects the mental faculties or moral character…orderly or prescribed conduct or pattern of behavior."[61]

That seems to be a good description of what we need in this country. Let's quickly look at some root cultural issues and check the application.

1. Would self-discipline help adults focus on alternative methods of satisfying our need for comfort rather than using food? Yep.

2. Would self-discipline help youth put education first, marriage second, and children third? Yep.

3. Would self-discipline help sexually active females to abstain from drining alcohol in order to prevent prenatal alcohol exposure? Yep.

4. Would self-discipline help our leaders in Washington become more outwardly focused and less inwardly focused? Yep.

But will they? Let me assure you that addressing the root issue is our best hope for a significant and sustainable impact. The implementation of self-discipline is a key, and there is a way.

I will begin by examining where self-discipline comes from. I will begin with these five:

1. Parents (especially fathers)

2. Faith

3. Mentors/Coaches

4. Military

5. Leaders

Perhaps you can identify with these five sources of self-discipline. Maybe you have more to add to the list. Let's look at what is happening to our sources of self-discipline in this country. Number one is *parents* and especially our dads. Remember chapter four? Forty percent of babies now come home without a committed father in the house.[62] That source of self-discipline is really taking a big hit. Number two is faith. According to *The Millennials*, 70 percent of Generation Y does not even consider religion to be relevant.[63] This is a concern. *Religion* is a form of core values. As we remember from chapter two, fracturing core values or the bedrock will result in eventual destruction. Number three is *mentors* and *coaches*. They are actually doing great in our nation. However, when it comes to sports, fewer teenagers are physically fit enough to participate. Number four is the *military*. According to a document signed by seven retired U.S. Army generals, only 25 percent of our young military-age men and women qualify to enter the military. Why? Problems with academics, physical fitness, or criminal records are keeping them out.[64] Number five is *leaders*. This is a mixed bag. Leaders in some institutions are doing well, and others are not. Overall, when we consider all five, I would say we are losing our sources of self-discipline.

So, if that is happening in our society, how do we turn it around? Considering we are on a tight time frame, we will need to look at the source we have the most control over, the source that can be changed in the shortest amount of time and that can be the most visible in our society. In my opinion, that would be number five, leaders. Since this book is focused mainly on social and political areas, I would recommend we consider the U.S. House of Representatives. We, the voters, do have control over electing this body, as difficult as it may seem. We can control the outcome collectively. Second, this body is elected every two years, so it is timely. Third, it is very visible to the public eye. If we want to improve the character and root issues in this nation, I would recommend the U.S. House of Representatives as the group of leaders to target.

RESEARCH

Well, this all sounds good, but is there any research to show that self-discipline as a character trait is important to political leadership? The answer is yes. Thanks to some digging by my daughter, who is a psychology major in college, and her professor, I will share with you the results of a study conducted over five years assessing the personality of the first forty-one presidents. It is called "Assessing the U.S. Presidents Using the Revised NEO Personality Inventory" and was written by Rubenzer, Raschingbauer, and Ones.[65] What is interesting to note about this research is the assessments are based on the five-year period before the individuals became presidents. All forty-one future presidents were assessed using the "Big Five Dimensions of (Global) Personality Ratings." The specific five are neuroticism, extraversion, openness to experience, agreeableness, and conscientiousness. The category with the highest mean score of the forty-one presidents was conscientiousness, with extroversion a close second. Each of the five personality categories was broken down into six facets. Like the others, the category of conscientiousness was broken down into six facets as well. The top three among the presidents were achievement striving, competence, and, yes, you guessed it, self-discipline.

President George Washington, for example, was literally off the charts in the category of conscientiousness. Consistent with the mean average of the other forty presidents, President Washington scored highest in the facets of achievement striving, competence, and self-discipline. The report went on to say: "Washington embodies the traditional virtues of duty, responsibility, self-discipline, leadership and courage. He falls quite short of the modern political commodities of warmth, empathy and open-mindedness." The report explained a low score on openness to values was an indicator that he was generally traditional in his morals and looked to leadership from church and religious figures in these matters.

One final note from the research on Washington is this: "When he turned in his commission at the end of the war, it was the first time in two thousand years that a victorious general did not seek political power as the result of his victory." The takeaway message here is there is precedence with high self-discipline in political leaders. It is part of being inwardly sound.

THE NEED

Perhaps for the first time in history, our nation is not being defended by a U.S. military at the front lines of a threat. Rather, it is being defended by a U.S. Congress. I say this only in the context of the national debt. Our military, the sector of society with the most discipline, is simply cheerleading while the U.S. Congress, the sector of society with a seemingly meager discipline, is fighting the battle for our nation's long term sovereignty. We cannot expect high school-level discipline to win at the professional level. Have we had good congressmen and women in the past? Yes. Do we have some good congressmen and women now? Yes. However the level of self-discipline that will be needed in the next decade is as high as any self-discipline that we have needed in the history of the nation. We have to be intentional. Your favorite candidate can commit to certain ideological views and promise to vote a certain way, right, left, or middle; but if he/she does not have the self-discipline to withstand the pressure, it does not matter how he/she line up with your views. If he/she cannot follow through for the long haul, what good does it do?

As a U.S. Congressional candidate, I filled out dozens and dozens of questionnaires about how I might vote, but nothing encouraged me or equipped me in the area of self-discipline. I realize self-discipline is not a precise science. It is a bit ambiguous. That is why it has not been dealt with before, but that does not diminish the need. You have heard it said, "We cannot expect to keep using the same approach and expect different answers." What got us into this mess will not get us out.

In chapter nine I will show you the specific solution for acquiring disciplined leaders. Before I describe the process, we have to check our assumptions. I have identified the need for leaders who are disciplined. I have identified the strong prevalence of self-discipline in past leaders. But is it really that important today? Maybe being outwardly focused is old school. Maybe it just sounds nice, and there is nothing in research to support this idea of *current* leaders being inwardly sound and outwardly focused. This assumption is so important that I am going to dedicate an entire chapter on the root of a leader. We cannot make an assumption here. We have to get this right before we can suggest any solutions.

ROOT LESSON FROM CHAPTER SEVEN:
Fixing half of something can
amount to nothing.

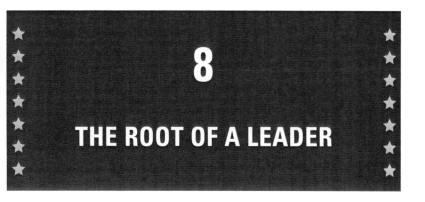

8

THE ROOT OF A LEADER

I just finished a ninety-hour work week. It was the most hours I had tallied for one week while serving a year in Iraq. It was Saturday night in a war zone, and I had made myself a promise that I was only going to put in four to five hours of work the next day and then rest a few hours, especially since it was Sunday. The next morning I awoke and put on the most casual clothes I could find in my CHU, or Containerized Housing Unit. Off to work I went with shorts and a T-shirt along with my DOD (Department of Defense) and State Department badges around my neck. I looked pathetic, but I needed to relax; I would keep a very low profile in the back of my office, which at that time was a tent in the back of Forward Operating Base Kalsu. I did not have any missions scheduled outside the wire into the red zone, so this should work.

Sure enough by midday, I had everything done I needed to do. Wait a minute. There was one more item on my list, and then I could rest the remainder of the day. I needed to get some copies made on the machine at the end of the hallway inside HQ (Headquarters). I wrestled with the idea of going into HQ with such casual attire. Finally I resolved in my mind that since it was Sunday, I could sneak in and sneak out quickly without much notice. The only person who might see me was the military personnel on duty at the front desk. I showed my DOD badge as I entered the building and proceeded back to the end of the hallway. I received a subtle look of disapproval at the front desk, which I was expecting anyway. Civilians embedded in the army have no rank to begin with, and I was approaching negative rank on that day. I completed the set of copies. All I had left was to walk down the hallway, and I'd be done!

Just as I entered my end of the hallway, I heard a flurry of activity in the building, and the whole place came alive. A contingency of people came directly toward me. As I was walking toward them, I recognized the person at the front of the group. *Oh no*, I thought. *That's General Petraeus.* It is everyone's highlight in a war zone to meet someone like General Petraeus or Condi Rice, but not today. Not in this situation.

All of a sudden, I could relate to women who say, "I don't even have on any makeup." For me, I was not in the correct attire. I certainly could not turn around and walk the other way. We were walking toward each other with nothing in between us but empty hallway. All of a sudden, he took a sharp left into the battle room along with his contingency. Thank God! As I walked by the battle room where all high level meetings occur, I could see my friend and coworker, Mike Maxey, who was inside preparing to brief the general along with the key military personnel from our base. Movements within the military are classified and can occur on very short notice. Mike found out just that morning he needed to brief the general later that day. I heard others say Mike did a great job, and I believe it. On my quick departure from the building, I found out we could come back in a couple of hours and attend a brief talk General Petraeus would be delivering to the general population. I will come back to the general in a bit.

I want to introduce you to the character of leaders in our military. There is a reason why the Harris Poll shows that our nation's confidence in our military leaders is 59 percent but only 8 percent confident in our congressional leaders.[66] Let me start with the commander and lieutenant commander of my brigade. Our commander's name was Colonel James and the lieutenant commander's name was Lieutenant Colonel Schuck. These two were not just leaders in name; they truly represented what leadership should look like. First of all, *they were in shape physically.* They both looked like soldiers. Second, *they led by example* and worked harder than anyone. They led the early morning briefings and were still working into the nights. Third, *they were courageous.* They were conducting more missions out in the red zone than anyone else. It was obvious they were inwardly sound and outwardly focused. Their self-discipline and character were tremendous.

Pictured left to right are Colonel James, 4th Brigade Commander of the 3rd Infantry Division; George Stickels, U.S.DA; Major Lazarz; and Lieutenant Colonel Shuck.

One of my first days on base, I went along on an all-day mission that Lt. Colonel Schuck was leading. While we were waiting in line to board two Blackhawks, he came over to me with a sympathetic smile on his face and said something to the effect of my "getting broken in quickly." He was right. I was green as grass and did not even know for sure how to buckle all the necessary straps after getting on a *bird*. A few months later, I was standing outside the HQ and talking to one of the convoy leaders for Colonel James, our brigade commander. I was shocked at the number of trips he was taking and the events he was attending.

Fourth, *these leaders were very engaged in their troops' morale.* Being concerned about the morale of the troops was one thing; being concerned for the morale of the civilians on base was something that was way above and beyond what was even thought of or expected. I will give you an example.

One day we were having a going-away ceremony on base to honor the work of the civil affairs team. It was later in the day. It was in early winter, and nights get cold in the desert. I did not have all my cold-weather gear out and washed for the first time. I grabbed an old long-sleeve shirt that was wrinkled and threw another short-sleeve shirt over the top. I was not participating in the event, and so I decided to dress down. Frankly, I looked a little sloppy...again. I thought I could get by with this dressed-down look for one night as long as I sat in the back. Near the end of the event, Colonel James came over from HQ and presented commander coins to those being honored. These coins are gold, numbered in quantity, and highly respected in the military. Near the end of the event, he said there were a couple more people he wanted to present commander coins to, and he turned and looked at me and asked if I would come up and receive a coin. *Oh no!* I thought. *Here we go again, totally underdressed for the occasion.* Despite this situation, he was very gracious and showed great concern for the morale of civilians on base. Wow! What great leadership.

The fifth and last trait I will list here is *humility*. A leader with a humble spirit attracts people who will follow that leader. It was easy to show my leaders respect, and their response was that of humility. Late in 2008, Lt. Colonel Schuck was one day away from going home or redeploying back to the United States. He yelled out my name from across the courtyard by the dining facility, or DFAC, and then walked over to give me a hug. I was not sure if you were supposed to hug commanders and lieutenant commanders in the army. But I guess you can when it is appropriate. These leaders knew all about being humble, and they also knew humility needed to be expressed at the right time and the right situation. Lt. Colonel Schuck and I went on to have a wonderful conversation about his rejoining his wife and kids when he got back to the States.

Another leader I will introduce you to briefly is General Smith. He was a one-star general with the Tenth Mountain Division. He and I co-facilitated a Credit and Jobs Roundtable held at Camp Victory west of Baghdad. Co-facilitating with a civilian was something he could have rejected. Instead, he treated the situation with great respect. We had an excellent event that I hope built relations among Iraqis and Americans. As busy as generals are in a war zone, he could have left that event behind but instead made sure to greet me a month later at another event. So, are these leaders in shape physically? Yes. Are they intelligent? Absolutely! But they also contain the character and self-discipline we all desperately want from our leaders.

General Smith of the 10th Mountain Division prepares for a Credit and Jobs Roundtable at Camp Victory, Iraq.

Let me go back to General Petraeus now. After his briefing inside HQ, he came outside and addressed the rest of us who were available. By the way, you will be happy to know I went back and dressed properly for this event. When he addressed the troops, he did not stand at a podium with grandeur; instead he stood on the ground in the middle of the troops and asked them to come in closer for a discussion. He showed tremendous respect for his troops as he presented commander coins to those with multiple tours. He demonstrated a refined, humble spirit in the way he conducted himself. I was impressed. One of his greatest virtues was his personal character. It is what you really hope for in a true leader. Just a few days later, I saw General Petraeus on TV giving a report to Congress in Washington, DC. He looked good! If you have been on a fourteen-hour flight, you know it will wipe you out. It takes a bit to get on your feet and running full strength. But there he was getting the job done with little evidence of fatigue.

General Petraeus, U.S. Commander in Iraq, delivers a speech before sunset at Forward Operating Base Kalsu.

General Petraeus, U.S. Commander in Iraq, takes time to provide commander coins at Forward Operating Base Kalsu to troops with multiple tours.

Later that year in 2008, General Petraeus was promoted to commander of Centcom or Central Command. In other words, he was the U.S. commander over a portion of the globe. His position as commander of Iraq was filled by General Odierno. By December of 2008, my brigade was redeploying home. I was transferred to the Regional Embassy in the ancient city of Babylon or modern day Al-Hillah, Iraq, to finish out my tour in 2009. On Christmas morning of 2008, I was in my office working on some diplomatic projects when our team was called into an immediate meeting down the hall. When we walked in the door, we found out General Odierno would be arriving momentarily. This time I was dressed right! Once again I could have had an excuse to dress down since it was Christmas, but I had learned my lesson. The general spent about an hour visiting with our small group, and then we went to the entryway for pictures. In these pictures, the general has a Santa hat on his head, with four stars on the front rightfully signifying his leadership status, but in a very humble manner. In the right time and in the right way, he was humbling himself on Christmas Day and took the time to lift the morale of the troops and civilians working in Iraq. Outwardly focused for sure!

Pictured left to right are Ken Hillas, Provincial Reconstruction Team Leader; General Odierno, U.S. Commander in Iraq; and Lieutenant Colonel Sias, Assistant PRT Leader. General Odierno demonstrated humility and concern for others on this Christmas morning 2008.

Outwardly focused leadership in the military is not exclusive to men. My second supervisor in Iraq was

Major Kimberly Peeples. She had a tremendous ability for bringing civilians and military personal together in a synergistic manner. This resulted in great working conditions and effective military outcomes. What always impressed my about Maj. Peeples was her strength and courage. Many weeks I would experience two or three missions outside the wire. Once outside the wire (our base), we had to be prepared for an attack at any moment. Many times the missions lasted all day in 110 to 120 degree heat while wearing body armor. Frankly, by the end of the week I was getting low on strength and low on courage. But not Maj. Peeples, she was always preparing for one more mission. She had great people skills and great courage at the same time.

Major Peeples, Assistant ePRT Leader, participates in a cornerstone ceremony near Forward Operating Base Kalsu.

Major Peeples, third from left, Mike Maxey, U.S.AID, center kneeling, and Steven Wilson, far right, with fellow members of the embedded Provincial Reconstruction Team at Forward Operating Base Kalsu.

Steven Wilson (civilian), second from left, stands with three brave soldiers after returning from a mission in Tunis, a city in Babil Province, Iraq.

My last supervisor before leaving Iraq in April of 2009 was Lt. Colonel Sias, another example of everything I have described in the other military leaders. He demanded respect but responded with a naturally humble spirit. He would never hesitate to seek us out in the dining hall to have lunch with his subordinates. He was always reaching for the Tabasco sauce and joking about this stuff being in his baby bottle when he was young. This is someone who had already served a tour in Afghanistan before this tour in Iraq. He never complained. He was a leader I could be around close-up day after day. His inner character was exceptional. This last leader in Iraq only confirmed my experiences with the inner character of the other military leaders I had witnessed. They were truly inwardly sound and outwardly focused.

Now I realize I have taken a long time to talk about the character of leaders in our military. My intent is to drill down to the root issue behind the confidence we have in our military and the lack of confidence we have in our U.S. Congress.

What did our founders say about the issue of character? As Samuel Adams, a signer of the Declaration of Independence, said: "The public cannot be too curious concerning the *character* of public men."[67]

Later in history, our twentieth president, James Garfield, said:

> Now more than ever the people are responsible for the *character* of their Congress. If that body be ignorant, reckless, and corrupt, it is because the people tolerate ignorance,

THE ROOT OF A LEADER

recklessness, and corruption. If it be intelligent, brave, and pure, it is because the people demand these high qualities to represent them in the national legislature.[68]

Sounds like something that we need to consider today. Or is it? Is there anything to back up this idea that internal character is important to be a *current* leader? Let's not make assumptions on such an important issue. This is where I will introduce you to a third Minnesota friend. His name is Tim Spiker. He has twelve years of experience researching the character DNA of leaders. His website called "Who* Not What" (whonotwhat.com) can help us answer this question of character in leaders. In the next few pages, I will share some of his comments with you from his website and, of course, with his permission. Here is Tim:

THE MOMENT IT
BECAME CLEAR

I stared at the whiteboard as if I expected it to move. My Atlanta office was nondescript, but the contents of my whiteboard were anything but that to me. I sat there pondering the leadership model on the wall. There was more to it than the colorful markings, but what was it? What was the truth beneath the surface of this picture? And then, it struck me. It felt as if a divine calling had simultaneously struck in my head, my gut, my soul, and my heart. It was so simple. It was so clear. How had I not seen it before?

A MISDIAGNOSED NATION | 181

I rushed down the hall to my mentor's office. Luckily, he was available. Fitting that I would be in his presence at this moment as he, more than anyone else I had ever worked for, encouraged me to press forward in this work even when my efforts were clumsy and complicated. I scribbled on his whiteboard as quickly as I could, writing illegible words that he knew only because of our countless previous conversations. With arrows and lines drawn so sloppily they could nearly be marketed as modern art, I shared the revelation. It was just three words: *who not what.*

THE HIDDEN TRUTH ABOUT LEADERSHIP

If you read nothing else, please read the next sentence. *Three quarters of leadership effectiveness is about who the leader is as a person rather than what the leader does.* That's it. That is the truth. But, we're blind to it much of the time. Whether we're watching the news or sports, reading blogs or the latest airport business books, listening to talk radio or podcasts, the issue remains the same: When it comes to leadership, we're almost always missing the real issues. We see ineffective leadership and attempt to address it far away from the source of its problems. We focus on new strategies, better execution, and the need to become more motivational without looking at whether or not the people behind those strategies, execution plans, and motivational messages are worth following. We're so focused on what we think leaders should be doing that we don't get around to addressing what makes up the vast majority of exceptional leadership: *who the leader is as a person.*

In its July 2008 publication, *The FMI Quarterly*, consulting firm FMI (www.fmi-net.com[69]) revealed the results of research it conducted using more than 20,000 leadership assessments. In search of a correlation between personality type, natural abilities, and leadership performance, FMI stumbled upon data that suggested that more than three quarters of a leader's effectiveness is attributable to his/her performance in just two of eight leadership categories. Within these two categories are ideals such as personal disciplines, integrity, authenticity, health and balance in all areas of life, self-awareness, a clearly understood sense of purpose, humility, emotional intelligence, and unconditional love (yes, *love*). Such ideals are, at their core, the essence of who a person is. They are the very foundation of what makes an exceptional human being. And yet, despite the significance of its discovery, FMI only describes these as the *behaviors and skills* of leaders, mere actions to be taken, and nothing deeper.

Sometimes the truth is right in front of us, and somehow, we miss it. That had been true of me for a long time. I had known about FMI's research long before they published it. I had been a consultant there for a number of years and was involved in the original research that served as the precursor to the data published in July 2008. But, it wasn't until long after I had departed FMI that the hidden truth beneath its research results revealed itself to me.

When the idea of Who* Not What first overcame me, I began testing it against what I had seen in all the leaders I had previously interviewed, coached, and observed. The idea held in every instance. Discussions with friends revealed the same, as did interactions with leader development colleagues. I finally turned toward my own experiences of being led. The examples supporting Who* Not What were clear and vibrant there as well. I simply couldn't find a spot where it did not hold true, at least not over the long haul of sustainable leadership.

ME AS A FOLLOWER: MY WHO* NOT WHAT STORY

Have you ever known about something long before you viscerally experienced it? You read books about the Grand Canyon before you go, but no book can prepare you for what you see when you get there. You watch college basketball on TV, but it's no comparison to being present for the rivalry game of your alma mater. You hear a friend's story about the poverty in India, but it can't prepare you for what you see when you are there. So it was with me and Who* Not What. I had just landed what I considered to be my dream job ten to fifteen years earlier in life than I ever thought possible. I was full of excitement as I packed up my car to move to Seattle, Washington, to work for a consulting firm based there. Within six months of the move, however, my excitement had worn off. Though I loved the content of my work, I found life at the firm very difficult. I felt unsupported. Numerous talented colleagues had left or were planning to leave. The culture within the company felt toxic, and our practice group within the firm experienced more of that toxicity than any of the other practices. In three short (or perhaps *long* would be a better descriptor here) years, we'd had no fewer than five different people lead our practice group.

Two of those five leaders transported me from head knowledge about Who*NotWhat to a visceral heart experience I will never forget. They led me in virtually identical circumstances: same clients, same work, same deliver mechanisms, same corporate cultures. The only thing truly different between my two experiences with them was which one of them was leading me. They provided me with two crystal clear examples, the truth of Who* Not What, both good and bad. For the sake of this printing I have changed their names to Roger Lathrop and Matt Sanders.

Roger Lathrop	Matt Sanders
Political Science, Harvard University Master of Liberal Arts UNC Asheville	Liberal Arts, Northern Iowa University Doctor of Jurisprudence, Loyola (Chicago) University School of Law
Spiritual Development Mentor, United States Naval Academy	Chief Legal Council, International Building Products Manufacturer
Managing Director, Boutique Consulting Group	Europe Division Executive VP and President, International Building Products Manufacturer
An exceptional public communicator and an acceptable business strategist	An acceptable public communicator and an exceptional business strategist
Chartered an entirely new method for consulting sales within the firm, landing the largest consulting engagements in the firm's history	Astute in acquisition deals

One of these men turned out to be the best leader I have ever worked for, and the other, one of the most challenging. Was it Roger or Matt who lost numerous subordinates while allowing an atmosphere of unrest to reign? Was it Roger or Matt for whom I would have done nearly anything to be under his leadership? Can you tell who is who from the information listed above? If you're like most people I've shared this story with, you're on the fence. Reading samplings of their accomplishments, positions, and skills provides little clarity as to whom was the exceptional leader and whom was the ineffective leader. But information of a different sort brings significantly greater clarity.

Roger Lathrop	Matt Sanders
During my first week of employment, left me to manage a room full of company presidents whom I had just met. Returned 15 minutes later whispering in my ear, "That's all the development you'll ever get from me."	Immediately ascertained I was unhappy after stepping into leadership and requested a meeting to hear my concerns and frustrations.
With a vacation that had been planned for a year beginning the following day, required that I cancel the vacation and work to fix a miscommunication issue for which he was the primary player. Then, before the end of the week, forgot that my vacation had been cancelled in order to fix the situation.	Rather than caving or throwing people under the bus, he made it his primary job to take heat on behalf of his subordinates when senior leaders did not understand the long term value his subordinates were creating for the company.
Never once admitted fault or any contribution to any difficulties that arose within a practice group or with clients.	Had a clear understanding of his personal shortcomings and shared them with the team.
Was uncertain about whether or not tell the truth to the Board of Directors when it came to their attention through back channels that I was leaving the firm. (He already knew I was leaving.)	When he was offered a dream job opportunity, called subordinates whom he had been leading to ensure they would be OK if he were to leave.

Now, guess who the exceptional and not-so-exceptional leader is? Pretty easy using this second table, isn't it? That is Who* Not What in action. The second table tells the leadership story much more than the impressive résumé snippets for both men included in the first table. After reading the second table, we intuitively understand whom we'd run through the proverbial wall for and whom we wouldn't. We don't have to explore the nuances of leadership to see who the better leader was. It is, in a word, obvious. The first table displays what these leaders did while the second displays who they were. Who, not what, determined how effective each leader was. At a gut level, we all get it.

I still remember the first one-on-one conversation I ever had with Matt. We'd just completed a practice group meeting where he was introduced as our new leader. We had the usual client review conversations, and afterward, he asked to meet with me about a key client. About thirty-seven seconds into the conversation, he said, "We can talk about the client stuff later. Tell me, how frustrated are you?" By the end of that conversation, I had discovered that Matt was a man worthy of trust. I decided to share with him something I hadn't shared openly with others: I was in the process of updating my résumé and planned to be actively searching for a job within a couple of weeks. He then asked me to hold off for a couple of months to give him a chance to make some changes. I agreed.

A year later, enjoying my work far more than I had for the first year, I got a call one night from Matt. He had a job offer that he was seriously considering, and he was calling me to talk about it. His description of the opportunity sounded like it was tailor-made for him: a familiar industry, a major leadership role, and significantly improved compensation. It was obvious he should take it. So, why was he calling me? He wanted to make sure I'd be okay if he took the job. That's right. Knowing how much support he was giving me and others behind the scenes, he wanted to make sure we would be okay if he left. That's the kind of person Matt was...and is.

THE CORE OF WHO* NOT WHAT: INWARDLY SOUND AND OTHERS FOCUSED

So, what makes up the "Who" in Who* Not What? Two key concepts: inwardly sound and others focused.

INWARDLY-SOUND

What do you think of when you think of a *sound* human being? If you're like me, you think of a person who is comfortable in his/her own skin, able to take criticism well, and grounded. Additionally, this is a person of high moral character and with a clear personal mission. This person is not easily rattled because the inner work of understanding and accepting one's self, faults and all, has been done. For the inwardly sound person, life is not a series of tests by which one must prove himself/herself worthy of breath. That question has already been answered in the affirmative. The inwardly sound person is secure, trustworthy, focused, disciplined, and self-aware.

OTHERS-FOCUSED

Who is on the mind of the leader each day? Is it success of self or the success of others? Is it the wants of self or the needs of others? The leader who is truly others focused is so as a way of life. He/she wakes up in the morning considering others. The fuel for being others focused is humility and love for others. Self is a secondary thought as much as possible. And when combined with being inwardly sound, being others focused creates an abiding connection between leaders and followers.

Take great care to remember that Who* Not What is steeped in *being*. While actions are the natural results of who a person is, focusing solely on actions as we evaluate ourselves and others as leaders does not tell the whole story. It would be a mistake to conclude that exceptional leadership is about acting as if one was inwardly sound and others focused. That type of effort has a short shelf life. Eventually, all of our *acts* are found out. And just like your gut told you exactly who the more effective leader was between Roger and Matt after reading about who they were, so too will you be able to spot a leader's efforts to *act* a certain way rather than simply *be* the person he/she is. To be an exceptional leader over the long haul, one must address thoughts and beliefs to *become* inwardly sound and others focused.

MISCONCEPTIONS ABOUT WHO* NOT WHAT

It is possible to hear the Who* Not What message, see the ideals contained within, and still come to some very erroneous conclusions. Let's take a look at two typical misconceptions about Who* Now What.

Misconception #1

"Who* Not What is simply about being a nice person. Be a nice person, and you'll be an exceptional leader." False.

Having high moral character is a key component of being inwardly sound and, thereby, an exceptional leader. But having high moral character is far more complex and developed than merely being *nice*. For example, being transparent and courageous are critical to high moral character. Transparency and courage are about being real, even when it isn't convenient to do so.

Oftentimes, such realness requires leaders to *stir the pot*, engaging in and even instigating difficult conversations and encounters. People who do such things aren't usually referred to as *nice*. They might be referred to as *annoying* or *upsetting*, but *nice* would not usually be a word used to describe that person. Courage and transparency are hallmarks of an inwardly sound leader.

For a second example of how *nice* is grossly insufficient for describing the Who* Not What concept, consider this: being a secure human being is far more about understanding who you are, why you're here, what your gifts and limitations are, and why you matter than it is about being *nice*. Because inwardly sound leaders understand the answers to some of life's big questions about self-worth and purpose, their leadership is not an activity aimed at consciously or unconsciously satisfying their insecurity. It is entirely possible to be *nice* and insecure simultaneously. Perhaps you've met such people. In search of security and acceptance, they are *nice* to everyone. But their leadership lacks the steadiness and confidence of a truly sound human being. There are plenty of *nice* leaders whose personal insecurities derail their leadership effectiveness on a regular basis. Being *nice* does NOT make someone inwardly sound.

Misconception #2

"So what you're saying is, all I have to do is be inwardly sound and others focused, and I will be an exceptional leader. Nothing else matters." False.

Who* Not What speaks to the core of exceptional leadership. Who a person is as a human being is the foundation of all other leadership activities, such as execution, strategy creation, motivation, talent development, and vision development. Who the leader is as a person determines if the lion's share of the leader's efforts, the "What" in Who* Not What, will be as successful as possible. Whether or not a leader is inwardly sound or others focused will have an enormous impact on the leader's long-term success, but those two characteristics do not comprise 100 percent of what makes up a truly exceptional leader.

CASE STUDY: JUSTIN, ALLEN, AND NATE

One Monday a few years ago, a close friend of mine named Justin texted me the following note:

> I am done with this. I just had our VP come in and ask me how my weekend was. I said "my 8 hours of cost accounting on Saturday was surprisingly painless," to which he

responded "I need you doing [expletive] sales not [expletive] cost accounting." What is sad is that in the office/business I am known for having the best relationship with him. I am the ombudsman for anything that needs to be transmitted to or from our VP.

To understand Justin's situation, let me share a little bit about him. He is incredibly book smart but also retains a common sense that is so solid that it is often annoying. He has risen in the ranks of his organization to be not only the sales leader on multiple continents, but also one who is pursued regularly by those in the manufacturing and accounting areas of his company. This is, in large part, due to his uncanny ability to connect with people beyond most anyone I have ever encountered.

Some time ago, I was in Central America with Justin. We were part of a small group of people visiting a rural community for a week, interacting with the children there through skits and sports. At one point, our entire group realized that Justin was nowhere to be found. No one panicked, but there was at least a bit of concern. After a few minutes, I saw out of the corner of my eye what looked like a small horse galloping by amongst the rays of sunlight and shadows of the forest. On that horse sat Justin. A few minutes later, he came walking back to our group. We inquired what had happened and Justin explained, far too matter-of-factly for the situation, that a local farmer had lost his horse and he (Justin) was simply helping him find it (thus, the galloping animal we had observed moments ago). And to punctuate the point of this story, (Justin's ability to connect with people), Justin had little to no formal training in the native language of the local farmer. Justin's combination of strategic and relational gifts is rare, and most business people who meet him quickly find themselves thinking about how Justin might somehow be a part of their team.

Now recall the first sentence of Justin's text: "I am done with this." How does someone with such talent end up so frustrated? Wouldn't those around him ensure that he had all the space and support he needed to flourish? Wouldn't they remember what they saw when they hired him and what they had experienced since his arrival? Apparently the answer is no. And to understand that answer, let's travel back in time a couple of weeks prior to Justin's text to me.

About two weeks previous to his text, Justin found himself, as he regularly was, invited to a meeting above his pay grade and formal title. He sat with the president, Allen, and vice presidents of his company discussing the organization's lack of ability to keep its manufacturing equipment running reliably. Sales and clients were being lost. In the midst of the discussion, Justin confronted Allen, who had promised months previously to free up some much-needed physical space in the manufacturing area. It was a simple commitment that required nothing more than a request to the maintenance department. Allen attempted to presidentially sidestep Justin's questioning, but Justin would not be denied. He continued to press Allen for renewed dates and commitments to free up the needed space. Allen finally (but ever so briefly) confessed that he was the bottleneck and summarily ended the meeting without any resolution. Allen was simply unable to be held accountable and deal with the most basic of confrontations. Despite his title of president, Allen was underdeveloped as a human being.

Now back to Justin's boss, Nate, the vice president mentioned in Justin's frustrated text message. For Justin's entire existence, Nate has been less than impressive. Nate's business trips around the globe were a major part of Nate's personal sense of self-worth. He plays the sad role of an aged man attempting to be an international playboy. He is careless with company funds used for personal expenses. Nate wouldn't exactly qualify as a strategic business mind or intellectual giant. His vice-presidential perspective on the business is no more complex than "sell, sell, sell." Beyond introductions to clients and instructing Justin on how to cheat on his expense report, Nate has nothing to offer Justin in terms of coaching, growth, and development.

It would be easy to point the finger at Nate in this story as the major problem and the reason for Justin's dissatisfaction. But he isn't first in line; Allen is. Allen's inability to handle confrontation is, first and foremost, the issue. This flaw, not in business strategy but in human development, is a major impediment to keeping talented individuals such as Justin in the organization. This underdeveloped aspect of Allen has existed for years. It is what has allowed Nate to operate as he has, out of control and unchecked. Justin's text, the true beginning of the end for him in this company, is fueled primarily by a lack of personal development by Allen. This is a perfect example of how who we are as people is responsible for three quarters of our success and failure as leaders. Who we are really matters when it comes to leadership. The impacts are not relegated to theory or philosophy. They are real. Just reread the first line of Justin's text to see it in action.

STILL NOT CONVINCED? LET'S LOOK AT YOUR STORY

Let's do a survey with a sample size of one. That one would be you. Take two minutes to make a list (no more than five) of the most positively influential leaders in your life. Ready, go.

If you're like most people, you didn't actually make the list. But if you had (and there's still time do it before you read on), you would most likely resemble many others who have done this exercise. You would have listed the names of parents, stepparents, high school teachers, junior-high sports coaches, aunts, uncles, clergy, older siblings, college advisors, and bosses encountered early in your career. And why did you write those names down? Did you write those names down because of their stalwart strategic capabilities? Or their excellence in producing quarterly profits? Or their skill in scheduling and project planning? Or their eloquence at a podium in front of hundreds of people? Highly unlikely. You wrote down most of the names you did because the leaders who made it onto your list took the time to care about you, your life, and where you were headed. You wrote their names down because they selflessly invested in you. They were authentic and honest with you. They cared more about what they were giving to the relationship than what they could extract from it. In short, you wrote down these names because of who these people were as human beings to you. This is the truth of Who* Not What in action in your life.

BEING ALL THAT YOU CAN BE

If we are to become the best leaders we can be, we must turn our attention away from mere strategy, execution, and, worse yet, the professional management of our images as leaders. Rather, we must turn toward the deep issues of who we are, first addressing if we are inwardly sound, then addressing if we are truly others focused. If we become inwardly sound and others focused, we will have mastered the foundations of great leadership. We will be trusted by followers and, most importantly, we will be worthy of that trust. It is through trust and committed followers that leaders accomplish great results, sometimes doing so with strategies and plans that are less than perfect.

It is a bit alarming to consider that we so easily allow others and popular media to tell us that exceptional leadership is defined as strategy, execution, and image management. We allow ourselves to be influenced into believing that the essence of leadership, the core of what creates deep and abiding followers that accomplish great things, is coming up with a great idea, pulling it off, and having people think well of the leader as it all happens. The data doesn't support that definition of exceptional leadership. My experience with Roger and Matt doesn't, either. Neither does your personal list of positive leaders. Over the long haul, we don't give everything we have as followers to support selfish egotists who are strategically brilliant. (Maybe, just maybe, we'd do that for a season, but not for a lifetime.) We give everything we have as followers to leaders who are inwardly sound and others focused. Those are the leaders who get the very best from us. Those are the leaders truly worth following, not because I said so, but because everything about us says so when we experience it. If we want to be the best leaders we can be, we'd

CHAPTER 8

all do well to focus our leader development efforts on what drives leadership effectiveness more than anything else; becoming the most inwardly sound, others focused leaders we can be; the best *Who* we can be. Exceptional leadership comes from who we are, not what we do. Who* Not What.

Some names and inconsequential details on the website have been changed to protect anonymity. All contents of this website are © The Tim Spiker Company. Inwardly sound, others focused, outwardly focused, who not what and Who* Not What are trademarks of The Tim Spiker Company.

These were insights from Tim Spiker. It looks like internal character has always been important and still is today. As a reminder, one of the items Tim mentioned was "others focused." In the social and political sense, we are concerned about both the voters and the nation. Therefore I will use "outwardly focused" in exchange for "others focused." They mean the same thing in this book.

One observation I want make about Tim's insights is this: the key element of being inwardly sound and outwardly focused is not a key element to profitability; it is a key element to effective leadership. Certainly they complement each other, but there is a distinct difference.

In chapters nine and ten, I will use inwardly sound and outwardly focused as key elements to the solutions.

★ ★ ★ ★ ★ ★ ★ ★ ★ ★ ★ ★ ★ ★

ROOT LESSON FROM CHAPTER EIGHT:
It starts with the heart.

★ ★ ★ ★ ★ ★ ★ ★ ★ ★ ★ ★ ★ ★

9

THE SOLUTIONS

This guy was really starting to upset me! After a few minutes it was clear, he was simply going through a laundry list of attempts to get money out of my pocket. Let's call this man "Mr. C." If I were to comply with all of his requests, I would need to write him a check for millions of American dollars on his way out the door. This guy had a different approach to hospitality than the other Iraqis I met. Overall, the hospitality of the Iraqi people was incredible. With the security and protection of the U.S. Army, I experienced meetings in the homes and businesses of dozens of Iraqi leaders. The gracious culture of the Iraqi people is revealed as rounds and rounds of tea, fruit, snacks, and sometimes main-course meals came our way. The relations were developing. Hearts and minds were being won in both directions. The Iraqi people were putting their faith in the American military to provide security for their nation while the Iraqis got their house in order under a new democracy.

However, as my year progressed, it seemed the meetings gradually were focused on more than just security. The Iraqis started looking for financial support or at least the desire for financial support from the

Americans. Mr. C. was the worst. He had determined in his mind that he would do everything he could to get as much money as possible out of the Americans before they left. I guess you could say he was an opportunist, at least from his perspective. He was only meeting for the money and the money alone. It was quickly becoming a habit for more and more Iraqis to look to the U.S. Army and the U.S. State Department for money. The continuation of this trend would not be good. It would result as an unintended consequence from governmental good intentions. We needed to head this problem off and soon.

My economic development team met to discuss the issue. We had a long meeting in front of a whiteboard on the military base. What can we do to help Iraqis move in the direction of being self-reliant rather than becoming addicted to our American support? As Americans, our intent was to find exit strategies, not create a monster attached to our hip. This was a war zone, and we needed to adjust to conditions daily. Fortunately, our economic team had the right talent to come up with a solution. We had brilliant minds from the officers of both the army and the Agency for International Development (U.S.AID). We developed a three-stage flow chart that illustrated the steps a nation takes when it is in a post-kinetic state. The tactic was to influence local Iraqi leaders through information. The third stage on the chart was the goal. It was simply titled "self-reliance." As Americans, we had to work our way out of a job in Iraq.

As we met with Iraqi leaders, we used this chart to show them the process of becoming self-reliant as a nation. We showed them that taking grants or too much money from the American government would not help them achieve the goal of self-reliance. It would only serve to move them away from self-reliance. The initial response from the Iraqis was mixed. They were not sure giving up that free money was the greatest idea they heard that day. I could understand their reaction. However, it was a start.

Now I have to stop and remind you that war zones are complicated. Some areas of Iraq were still very active with insurgents, and this approach would have been premature and counterproductive in those areas. However, our province where we were positioned was at the perfect stage for this tactic and curriculum. Soon after we created the chart, I transferred to a regional embassy in the same province, which gave me even more access to Iraqi leaders.

In the last three months of my tour, I had the fortune of meeting regularly with a group of outwardly focused leaders. This was perfect. They caught the long-term intent of the self-reliance chart. In the long run, it was good for Iraqis and good for Americans. Now, had this team consisted of a room of Mr. Cs, the result would have been entirely different.

By the time I left Iraq, the outwardly focused team of Iraqi business leaders embraced the vision and the approach to achieve self-reliance. I remember sitting in the last major meeting between these Iraqi leaders and a key U.S. army general before the end of my tour.

During the meeting two leaders from the local Iraqi group stood up and announced that they were no longer interested in grants and money from the Americans. They wanted to focus their attention on different areas, such as technical assistance. I was about ready to jump out of my seat and say, "Wahoo!" But that would not have been part of the Iraqi culture. Instead I sat quietly in my chair with a huge smile on the outside and a feeling on the inside that a mission had been accomplished. We had only impacted one province of Iraq, but it was the area we had responsibility to influence. America would very likely provide technical assistance such as security training and agriculture production. At least within this specific group in this region, Iraq and the U.S. were now on the same page both militarily and diplomatically. Now we both had the same vision and approach in mind.

In all, I have worked in five foreign nations spanning thirty years. The work ranged from one week to one year in length. Four of the five situations involved nation-building. In the context of this chapter, I will share two lessons. First, it is possible to have influence without large, direct government handouts. I have personally experienced this; first, in the former Soviet bloc countries; second, working with the U.S. government here in the States; and third, with Iraqi leaders. It takes more work, but the results will be long lasting. The second lesson is this: in order to accomplish a crucial mission with limited time, you have to find inwardly sound and outwardly focused leaders to carry out the mission. From my work with Eshtvan in the former Soviet bloc countries in chapter two up to the Iraqi leaders in this chapter, it was outwardly focused leaders who got the job done right. I will apply both of these lessons to the two solutions I will identify in this chapter. The first solution will focus on social issues. The second solution will focus on political issues.

Before we dig into these two solutions, we do need to check our assumptions. So here is the question of the day: is it the federal government's job to fix root issues? Hmm. It does cause one to pause for a moment. That could turn into an ideological debate all in itself. Is it possible that one root issue could be the responsibility of the federal government and another one might *not* be the responsibility of the federal government? What about a root issue that falls within a state? The answers might be entirely different with state governments. There may be some who would ask if even some surface issues are the responsibility of the government, such as diets and nutrition. I have boxed myself into a corner now because I am going to have to take a stand in order to move forward with this chapter. To help me do this, I will reflect on the Constitution.

The Preamble of the Constitution acts as a type of vision statement for the purpose of the Constitution and the federal government. The founders chose their words very carefully. The preamble says that we should "provide for the common defense" and "promote the general welfare." For most, it is easy to understand the difference in terminology. We absolutely provide the military for our nation. "Promoting" in this constitutional context refers to something different than providing. Promoting refers to setting up fair rules for someone else to do the providing. If there is any question about this, we can refer to Article One, Section Eight of the Constitution, where the founders give seventeen specific examples. The word "provide" is used in the context of enforcing the law domestically and defending the nation internationally. Promoting is referred specifically in the context of fair rules for the people, such as copyrights and patents. This line between providing and promoting has been blurred over time, and some would consider it regressive at this point to follow a strict constitutional line. Let's tidy that line up a bit in a way that follows the Constitution but does not regress in our fight against social issues. This will be one of the objectives of our solution for root social issues.

Back to my question of the day. For the reasons I have stated, it is clear that *it is not the role of the federal government to fix root issues.* If it is not the responsibility of the federal government to fix root issues, whose responsibility is it? Here is where I will stay off the fence and follow a root-issue in harmony with the U.S. Constitution. In this chapter, I will demonstrate how the federal government can "promote" the fixing of root issues without being directly involved. The federal government will promote an environment for someone else to do the providing. Ultimately the solution needs to point back to the people as the responsible party. Even if we believe it is the role of the federal government to fix root social issues, we get caught with the next assumption. That assumption is this: Our good government intentions will turn into good results without any consequences. My experience and opinion is the federal government has good intentions that too often result in unintended consequences, especially in root issues. I am going to walk you through a specific example to help demonstrate this idea. This example should clearly show it is not the role of the federal government to fix root issues.

As I discussed in chapter four, fatherless homes are a root cause of crime. Mentoring can be an effective means of providing additional one-to-one nurturing when the parent is not available. It would make sense then why the federal government would get directly involved with funding mentoring programs for children of prisoners. Some would call it a no-brainer. So, that is exactly what the federal government did. The HHS (Department of Health and Human Services) funded a program for mentoring children of prisoners in 2002 under the Bush administration. I became directly involved with the federal program in 2003. I applied for funding with the HHS on behalf of our nonprofit to receive federal dollars for the program in Minnesota. The nonprofit was awarded a grant of $450,000 over three years.

WHAT HAPPENS TO YOUR TAX DOLLAR?

First, we will look at the financial efficiency of the program. Let's follow the dollar as it left your pocket and went into our nonprofit. You file your taxes with the IRS and send or receive money back from the U.S. Treasury. A little less of your dollar is appropriated by the U.S. Congress to the executive branch of the federal government. In this case the HHS is one of the departments of the executive branch. The HHS has a division called Administration for Children and Families, or ACF. The HHS passes a little less of your dollar down to the ACF. The ACF has a bureau called the Family and Youth Services Bureau or FYSB. The ACF hands a little less of your dollar down to FYSB. The Family and Youth Services Bureau conduct a competitive RFP (Request for Proposal) process which can last for a year. The awardees receive their money when it is available from the PMS or Payment Management System. The PMS processes a little less of your dollar through the ACH or Automated Clearing House. And eventually it is deposited in the bank account of the nonprofit. I honestly cannot tell you how much of your dollar got back to the nonprofit, but we can safely say it was much less than a dollar. Therefore, efficient use of money should be a consideration in the solution I am about to show you.

BUREAUCRACY

But wait ... there is more to consider. Awardees are required to fill out and process lengthy reports on three different levels at different intervals with different people. Awardees have a case manager to answer questions as they arise. Some of this does happen, but what is surprising is the awardees also *report* to the same case manager. For example, the case manager can contact the awardees without warning and request random reports that are due in a matter of days. In addition, regular training is required in Washington, DC that may include training that was covered the year before. Some

208 | STEVEN J. WILSON

of the bureaucracy is needed, but it certainly would be better if the bureaucratic process could be reduced or avoided entirely. Reduced bureaucracy should be considered in the solution I am about to show you.

RESULT

The federal government now evaluates many of their own programs. The evaluations are done through the Office of Management and Budget (OMB) and can be viewed at ExpectMore.gov. The programs are rated and placed in two basic categories: performing programs and nonperforming programs. As of 2011, "Mentoring Children of Prisoners" was rated as a nonperforming program.[70] Here we have years of work from people all over the United States spending hundreds of millions of federal dollars, and in the end, it is deemed a nonperforming program. What creates the drama here is that mentoring is a well-researched and recognized effective approach for improving root issues with youth. What went wrong? Clearly this is a case in point of what happens when the U.S. government steps over the line from "promoting" to "providing" the general welfare. Indeed this is only one example of the federal government's attempt to fix root social issues. However, in my opinion, it does demonstrate inefficiency and ineffectiveness. Good intentions can be expensive if they are conducted in the wrong place with the wrong provider.

So, why didn't President Bush's Faith-Based Initiative work well? It's simple. Many of the participating programs changed priorities. Prior to the federal funding, the priority would have likely been quality of service. Once the government funding started, the priority was all about quantity more than quality. Specifically it was about the number of people participating in the program first and the quality of the programs was pushed to second place. In other words, many faith-based organizations went from second gear to high gear in a short period of time, and quality suffered.

DEFINITION OF TERMS
As you read through this chapter, you are encountering some new terms. We need to define those terms.

Surface Organizations
As the name implies, surface organizations are those that generally deal with the surface issues. The most well-known surface organization is the U.S. federal government. Other surface organizations may be private nonprofits that focus on surface issues such as food and clothing.

Root Organizations
Root organizations are less common. A specific example of a root organization that you are familiar with comes from this book. Chapter five was written by Jody Allen Crowe, who is the founder of Healthy Brains for Children, an excellent example of a nonprofit that deals with root issues in our society. The organization creates public awareness of fetal alcohol exposure and the permanent risks that come from alcohol consumed during pregnancy. In Jody's book *The Fatal Link,* he clearly demonstrates this syndrome as a root cause of school shootings in America.

Other types of *root* organizations might be churches and faith-based nonprofits. One example of a faith-based root organization is the Inner Change Freedom Initiative which has had tremendous success in the reduction of recidivism, the return of former inmates, around the nation. Any nonprofit with programs that strive for good core values of adult prisoners and at-risk youth could be considered root organizations. Specifically, organizations that promote and focus on a strong self-image and healthy relationships with fathers are good examples.

Surface and Root Organizations

These organizations may be more prevalent than we think. These are organizations that focus on both surface and root social issues. The largest surface and root organization that I am aware of is the Salvation Army. This is an organization that deals with the surface issue of food and at the same time teaches good core values and promotes strong self-image in the same building. Almost every large metro area has surface and root organizations.

History of Surface versus Root Organizations

Before the 1900s, the federal government had little to do with surface issues or root issues in the social arena. The private sector through the local church and a budding Salvation Army along with other similar programs was all that the nation offered for social root issues. State governments, however, were involved in surface issues. One example is education.

OBJECTIVES OF THE SOCIAL SOLUTION

The first solution in this chapter will focus on the social root issues in America. It will accomplish six objectives:

1. Allow harmony with the U.S. Constitution—"Promote" the general welfare.

2. Allow the responsibility of the *root* issues to be on the people and away from the government.

3. Refrain from direct federal government hand-outs with root social issues.

4. Encourage an environment of being outwardly focused.

5. Refrain from "pruning the problem" (Chapter Seven).

6. Avoid being regressive in our actions with social issues as a whole.

A ROOT SOLUTION FOR SOCIAL ISSUES

For ease of terminology, let's call this root solution "Donor Dollars." Donor Dollars from this point forward is the name of the specific social-root solution we have been leading up to in this chapter. Here is how it works. Each year Congress would allocate a certain amount available to taxpayers that would reduce their taxes. It would not reduce a percent of the taxes. It would reduce the taxes dollar for dollar. This is called a tax credit rather than a tax deduction. Let's say that every tax payer is allowed 100 Donor Dollars. You as a taxpayer could reduce your federal taxes by donating money to qualifying nonprofits. In this situation you could donate $100 and reduce your taxes to the federal government by $100.

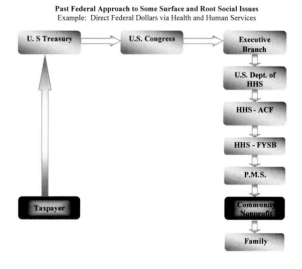

Past Federal Approach to Some Surface and Root Social Issues
Example: Direct Federal Dollars via Health and Human Services

Proposed Donor Dollars Approach to Some Surface and All Root Social Issues

Let's walk through an example. It starts with shopping. You live in a state where prisons are the fastest growing expense in your state's budget, and you decide it is a cause you would like to support. You shop for a nonprofit that has demonstrated results in reducing prison reentry, and you give $50 to them. Perhaps you are also concerned about the effects of fetal-alcohol exposure to babies in our nation. You could donate the second half of your money or another $50 to a different nonprofit that has a proven track record with educating youth about fetal alcohol syndrome. In other words, you would find a nonprofit you deemed effective and donate your money directly to the nonprofit. The first $100 dollars would be taken off of your federal tax liability for that year. It is that simple. The decisions are 100 percent transferred to the taxpayer. It is your decision and yours alone. At least 50 percent of those Donor Dollars would need to be donated to nonprofits located inside your home state. The remaining Donor Dollars could be spent inside your state or nationally.

State governments could also participate in Donor Dollars by adding to the program beyond the federal government's $100. For example, the state could allow $40 of Donor Dollars at the state level for a grand total of $140 Donor Dollars. If the state was struggling with a specific social issue, they could also target the state Donor Dollars if they so choose. I would encourage states to only target Donor Dollars as an exception. If the Donor Dollars are targeted on a regular basis, special interest money will start flowing and start controlling the targets.

Qualifying Nonprofits

The nonprofits would qualify for Donor Dollars by demonstrating the following:

1. The nonprofit has fully completed the tax-exempt review period and has received their final determination letter from the IRS.

2. The nonprofit would need to clearly identify the first two purposes of the nonprofit as listed in their application for tax exempt 501(c)3 status with the IRS. Those two purposes would need to be part of the Donor Dollars program to qualify. In other words, a nonprofit art museum cannot receive Donor Dollars intended for at-risk youth.

Savvy Shoppers

The people have now been empowered to address the root social issues of this nation. The hope is that savvy shoppers for nonprofits will seek to diversify their portfolio. They will point their Donor Dollars in the direction of root organizations and root solutions as much as surface organizations and surface solutions. Here is one reasonable question about Donor Dollars. Will taxpayers forget about the program? The answer is no. The nonprofits will have major campaigns making sure those Donor Dollars are used by savvy shoppers.

Price Tag

The cost of the Donor Dollars could be a very small portion of the social entitlement programs.

Implementation

The Deming philosophy of process improvement is that of Plan Do Study Act.[71] This means plan the program, do the program on a small scale, study the areas for improvement, then act on a larger scale. This is always a good approach to a new initiative.

Advantages of the Donor Dollars

- 100 percent Efficient Process

  All of your money actually arrives at the non-profits rather than a percent of your money. In other words, we can increase dollars into the social needs of our nation without increasing taxes.

- 100 percent Citizen Control

  The citizens have control of the Donor Dollars, not special interest groups.

- More Efficient Nonprofits

  The nonprofits can focus fundraising on traditional methods with the people rather than redirecting management time to courting the federal government.

- Agility of Programs

  Having the focus at the local level will allow changes to be made by nonprofits day by day to respond to the social needs rather than waiting for annual program adjustments to be made in Washington D.C.

- Root Issues Promoted

  Nonprofits that focus on root issues will have a much better chance of receiving Donor Dollars or support than the previous method of government support.

- Open the Door for Volunteers

  There is a false perception by the public with the current system. If the government is directly responsible for a wide range of social issues, there is a perception that the government is responsible and I am not. I do not need to donate to nonprofits because the government must have a program. Or, I do not need to volunteer with a nonprofit because the government must have somebody working with these issues. The unintended consequence of the government being directly involved with social issues is a breakdown between prospective volunteers and the nonprofit. The perception is the need is being met. There is a false perception that my hour of volunteering is not vital since the government takes care of those needs. The Donor Dollars program opens the door again for more potential volunteers.

I am sure I can come up with a few more advantages, but I hope you can see a clear difference with the Donor Dollars approach.

Now that we have identified a better solution for *promoting* the general welfare, especially with root issues, let's take it for a test run. This approach actually happened, in part, to Bridge Builders for Kids, the nonprofit my family founded in the year 2000. The tax credit part of Donor Dollars did not happen, but the other parts did happen. Bridge Builders has grown from summer camps for children of prisoners to parenting classes for parents coming out of prison. Bridge Builders for Kids, or BBFK, was just starting a class for fathers preparing to be released from a Minnesota Department of Corrections facility in 2011.

Right before the first class, state budget cuts came into play, and the state funding for the program was frozen. The executive director of BBFK, Jeff Bremer, sent an e-mail to the MN Department of Corrections and asked if the DOC would move forward as planned with the classes if the nonprofit could raise the money from the private sector. A few days later, Jeff received an e-mail back saying, "Let's move forward!" Did you catch that? It was like driving through a town of fifty people.

I will recap, as it all happened too quickly. First, there was a qualified nonprofit available. I define qualified because it has a 501(c)3 status from the IRS with a final determination letter in hand. Second, there was a preexisting relationship between the nonprofit and the social need. In this case it involved a state government entity. Funding was needed to move the social program forward. One e-mail was sent from the nonprofit to the government entity consisting all of thirty-three words. A response was sent back five days later. The e-mail response from the government to the nonprofit consists of twelve words. So, in five days and forty-five words, a social need was met. Conditions were changing on the ground, and the nonprofit had the agility to shift gears and respond. As I am writing this book, the first class actually took place three days ago with private funding. The classes are vital as the inmates being released will need access to training for reuniting with their children. Now a lot of details will follow, but take a look at how easy it can be. The bureaucracy just left the house, so to speak. This type of approach can happen all over America if the federal government would simply set up a Donor Dollars program. The Donor Dollars will only pay for a portion of these social needs, but it will go a long way to get donors connected with nonprofits, and then let the donors and nonprofit finish the job themselves. The federal government just "promoted" the idea of you getting involved. The federal government "promoted" the idea of you providing for the general welfare of the nation.

What does the agility of the nonprofit mean to you and society as a whole? In the example above, one the strongest influences for keeping an inmate from re-offending is a strong relationship to their family. When that family relationship is strengthened, it can mean fewer taxes to pay for prisons. Most importantly it improves the chances of the children of the inmate to have a stronger self-image from the positive relationship with the father. The stronger self-image will decrease the chances of Junior following in his dad's footsteps in and out of prison.

The last thing I will mention in using Donor Dollars is this: the whole environment changes when you move away from the federal government to the private nonprofit sector. Just think about it. When you are asked by the federal government to get involved with a social need, you think about making money. When you are asked by a nonprofit to help with a social need, you think about donating your time. This is a paradigm shift in seconds from being inwardly focused to outwardly focused. Dwell on that idea for a bit.

I hope you can see this solution will meet all six objectives set forth earlier in the chapter.

Now we will move on to the second solution in this chapter.

A ROOT SOLUTION FOR POLITICS

Let's quickly review the root issue of the national debt from chapter six. We determined that the root cause of our national debt is a Congress that is inwardly focused. Remember the top five priorities of Congress?

1. My Election

2. My Party

3. My Special Interest Groups

4. The Voters

5. The Nation

This has been the case for a long time and makes it difficult to fix. As we discussed in chapter two, these types of behaviors start out as an idea, grow to action, grow to a habit, grow to a behavior, and then become part of the culture. Unfortunately, when it becomes part of the culture, it is no longer viewed as bad but part of business. So it is with Congress. They have had the first three priorities in place for so long that it is no longer seen as bad. After a while, even a skunk smells good to himself. Society tolerates this political culture until number one and number five are in direct conflict with each other, and that is where we are today. The only way to fix the root issue is to change the culture of the House and Senate to a genuinely outwardly focused body of Congress. We need a majority of the members and the president. A big task? Yep. This nation has plenty of big tasks, and it is up to the people to do something about it.

The good news is we have a time-tested model to follow. Remember the numbers from the Harris Poll? The confidence in the leaders of Congress was 8 percent, and the confidence level of our military is 59 percent.[72] What is the difference? As chapter eight demonstrates at the core, the military is outwardly focused, and chapter six shows us that Congress at the core is inwardly focused. Chapter eight goes on to identify that being inwardly sound and outwardly focused provides 75 percent of what creates effective leadership. Again, the military has a 59 percent confidence rating, and it is outwardly focused. Congress is inwardly focused and has an 8 percent confidence rating in leadership. So, how do we fix the root issue of the national debt for the long term? It is a lot easier once you know the root issue. It comes back to the courage of the people to carry it out and the willingness to sacrifice for our nation. In this case, will the people organize the solution and will candidates sacrifice a few days of time for the interest of the nation? The enemy is obvious. It is an inwardly focused culture in the political system.

As we identified in chapter seven, we will specifically target the U.S. House and then the Senate. The mission is clear. We the people need to shift the political culture in the U.S. House from being inwardly focused to an outwardly focused culture. It has to occur with 51 percent of the U.S. House, or 218 people. That's it. That is the mission. It may be an unconventional mission, but it attacks the root.

The mission is not to blow up a building on a foreign land. It is to change a culture on our land by influencing leaders with information, the same as we discussed at the beginning of this chapter. There may already be 100 members of the U.S. House that are devout in being outwardly focused. They are in desperate need of reinforcements. We the people are responsible to send those reinforcements. We need to create a culture around 218 people who are willing to sacrifice for their nation. These 218 will not lose their lives, but they need to be willing to lose their own next election if that is what is needed to put our nation on a sustainable path financially. We need patriots who are willing to lose their next election if that's what is needed to give our children and grandchildren the same opportunities we had in this nation; they need to be willing to lose their next election if that is what it takes to preserve "the shining city on a hill."

IMPLEMENTATION

So, how do we accomplish this mission? We have the time-tested model of the military that still works today. In order for the military to work, each member of the military begins their adventure with something called boot camp. Some would say it tears a recruit down and builds a soldier up. They walk out with root issues addressed such as behavior and core values. Both of these two root issues are meant to be enhanced through the boot-camp experience. Some of those core values are self-discipline, selfless service and respect for authority, and respect to the point of obedience. The ultimate goal is for the new soldier to be inwardly sound and outwardly focused.

This is the same process we need in our Congress. We need a boot camp for Congress. The objective is to turn out new candidates and incumbents who are inwardly sound and outwardly focused. The boot camp should end with the candidates and incumbents signing pledges to be outwardly focused. This idea comes from the signers of the Declaration of Independence, "…we mutually pledge to each other our Lives, our Fortunes and our sacred Honor."[73] In the same way, the graduates of this congressional boot camp will sign a pledge that is relevant to today. The graduates' pledge would simply include a commitment to switching priorities one and five described at the beginning of this solution. The boot camp may only last two to three days. Evening speakers could be military leaders such as military generals who have walked the talk in being outwardly focused. The curriculum during the day would revolve around the Who* Not What approach as described in chapter eight. Historical examples would be taught demonstrating true sacrifice of those congressional leaders serving in the past. Just as soldiers are required to come back for a regular physical exam of doing pushups and running, congressional boot camp graduates who have attended Who* Not What in the past would voluntarily attend future refresher courses. A website for the congressional boot camp would list graduates. Their respective pledges would be posted on the Internet for voters to read. The boot camp would be funded entirely by private funds combined with registration fees. The candidates and incumbents would attend voluntarily. You, the citizens in their district or state, will influence their attendance. A copyright-protected outline of the Who* Not What curriculum would be provided online at the boot-camp website for transparency purposes. Eventually the boot camps could be available monthly during the election year itself. The boot camp would continue until the mission is accomplished. "Ask Not" could be the theme or slogan of the camp, honoring the famous words of President Kennedy.

ESTABLISHING THE BOOT CAMP

There is a lot of precedence for establishing these types of endeavors. For example, think-tank organizations have been used for decades in America. These think tanks use information for the purpose of influencing the culture. One example is the Concord Coalition. I use the Concord Coalition[74] as an example because of *who* set it up. As is typical with many of these endeavors, its establishment included two former congressmen. In the case of the Concord Coalition, it was founded in 1992 by the late former senator Paul Tsongas (D-Mass.), former senator Warren Rudman (R-N.H.), and former U.S. Secretary of Commerce Peter Peterson.

The congressional boot camp will be developed and brought together by a board of former congressmen, women, and grassroots volunteers from both sides of the aisle. The former congressional members would be selected based on their history of demonstrating an inwardly sound and outwardly focused approach to politics. Other members of a founding board should include military leaders. I would suggest from a practical standpoint that a boot camp be available for Democrats and Republicans to attend separately. We cannot afford to have political party be the very thing that prevents the boot camp from happening. We need to meet people where they are in life. Both boot camps would have the same material and curriculum.

COMPARISON OF SURFACE SOLUTIONS VERSUS ROOT SOLUTIONS

Now that we have identified what we believe to be a valid solution for the root issue of the national debt, we need to compare it to the surface solution.

In December of 2009, and excellent report called "Red Ink Rising" was issued by many of the leading economists in the nation.[75] It outlined some excellent solutions to the surface area of the national debt. It recommended decreasing the forecasted deficits by 5 trillion during the time period 2012 to 2018. The goal was to reach 60 percent debt held by the public (as a share of GDP) by fiscal year 2018. Obviously, this is just a bit different than the root solution of implementing the Who* Not What philosophy into Congress. Keep in mind, a better diagnosis from chapter seven articulates that we must address both the surface and root issues in order to successfully complete the mission. On the surface level of budgets, we need to see plans such as "Red Ink Rising" introduced by Congress, and at the same time, we need to address the root issue of establishing an outwardly focused Congress as we just described. One will depend on the other.

SUMMARY OF SOLUTIONS

I currently own Unity Consulting Group, LLC, which is a small consulting firm focused on short and long-term business strategies. In 2011, I spent a day touring businesses in the Midwest with a client. The objective of the tour was to look at businesses similar in nature to my client's business and try to discover keys to the successful strategies. The timing was very interesting, as three of these businesses had lost money through the recession and then found ways to make money again. What I learned that day was this: all three did indeed cut some fat from their organization; however, all three stopped before cutting into the bone, if you will.

Instead, all three enacted a paradigm shift. In other words, before compromising any of the quality of their core business, they focused on a mindset change in how they did business.

I will give you an example. One business made a paradigm shift in their approach to managing staff. They had a couple of bad apples in the group that had been with the company for a long time. These bad apples were subtle in creating a negative mindset with the other employees. Management terminated the bad apples and created an environment of empowerment with the other staff members who remained. Gradually productivity improved along with the efficiencies, and finally the profit improved dramatically. Before making the paradigm shift, the company had lost $281,000 in one year. After the paradigm shift, they started making money again, and in 2011, the company was on track to generate a 5 percent net margin. Instead of compromising the quality of their product, they first turned to a paradigm shift in their thinking and approach to the business.

A second example we saw that day was a business that completely changed their approach to managing their facilities. This second business embraced some out-of-the-box approaches to their real estate, and it was working. The third business completely changed the management structure itself. Again, before compromising quality, all three first turned to a paradigm shift in their thinking and approach to the business.

We can learn from these lessons. As we approach solutions for the public sector issues, we can learn from successes in the private sector where troubled water has been turned into smoother sailing. If we act quickly, the public sector can avoid compromising the core of our nation and instead consider a paradigm shift in how we think about and approach our government.

I am going to end this chapter with an executive summary of a strategy for the United States. The summary will introduce a couple of paradigm shifts in how we think about and approach our social and political issues. Ultimately the executive summary is a collection of ideas from this book up to this point.

EXECUTIVE SUMMARY

The objective of this executive summary is to provide a strategy that will allow a sustainable long-term environment for the United States of America. The strategy will include:

1. Paradigm shifts

2. Consideration of both root issues and surface issues

3. Following the U.S. Constitution with respect to "providing" and "promoting"

The approach will be a chronological table of events.

YEAR	EVENT	DETAIL	OBJECTIVE
2012	Congressional Boot Camps	Chapter nine with support from chapter eight	Begin the transfer of an inwardly focused political culture to an outwardly focused political culture
2012	Pass and sign into law an SPA or Sovereignty Protection Act	Chapter six	Create a framework to address the national debt and protect the nation
2012	Initiate a pilot version of the Donor Dollars program	Chapter nine with support from chapters three, four and five	Address both root and surface *social* issues
2013	Congressional Boot Camps for Incumbents	Chapter nine with support from chapter eight	Continue the transfer of an inwardly focused political culture to an outwardly focused political culture
2013	Continue reform of discretionary and entitlement programs	Chapter six	Address the surface issues of our national debt
2013	Study the pilot version of the Donor Dollars program	Chapter nine	Move from the "Do" stage of Plan, Do, Study, Act and into the "Study" stage
2014	Congressional Boot Camps for incumbents and challengers in both the House and Senate	Chapter nine with support from chapter eight	Continue the transfer of an inwardly focused political culture to an outwardly focused political culture
2014	Completion of the pilot program for Donor Dollars	Chapter nine	Move from the "Study" stage of Plan, Do, Study, Act and into the "Act" stage
2014	Pass the permanent version of the Donor Dollars program	Chapter nine with support from chapters three, four and five	Continue with the "Act" stage of Plan, Do, Study, Act.
2015	Congressional Boot Camps for incumbents and challengers in both the House and Senate	Chapter nine with support from chapter eight	Continue the transfer of an inwardly focused political culture to an outwardly focused political culture
2015	Complete all permanent reforms to discretionary and entitlement programs	Chapter Six	Address the surface issues of our national debt
2016	Many Congressmen and Congresswomen will likely be voted out of office after serving only one or two terms	Chapter six and nine	Self-sacrifice for the good of the nation

Mission accomplished.

The only outstanding root issue we have not addressed in the executive summary is the voters' willingness to sacrifice. Will citizens be willing to sacrifice for the good of the nation? It's up to you. At the end of chapter ten we will cover one last solution and it will include you and what will hopefully lead to transformation.

SOLUTION CONCLUSION

So there you have it. We have gone full circle from chapter one. We started the book introducing the concept of root issues and the importance of maintaining a foundation of strong core values. We are now ending the book with prescribing a strategy for reestablishing strong core values in our social and political arenas.

In the social arena, we already have a strong contingency of inwardly sound and outwardly focused people assembled in our nonprofit sector. Donor Dollars will "promote" a foundation needed to expand their work.

In the political arena, we lack the number of individuals who are inwardly sound and outwardly focused. Creating a new culture will be difficult. The congressional boot camp is the place to start.

In chapter ten, I will discuss the root philosophy used as a foundation for this book and then hit the touchy issue of faith and its influence on root issues. Here is one final twist. In every chapter, I began with a story that relates to the contents of the chapter. In the next and final chapter, I will end the chapter with a story that summarizes the book.

THE ROOT LESSON FROM CHAPTER NINE:

It is not someone else's responsibility.

10

THE SUMMARY AND THE TRANSFORMATION

We have a lot to cover in this chapter. I will touch on the philosophy of this book. I will introduce you to a root model that will summarize core tenets of individuals and leaders discovered through this book. I will provide a summary of my root issue findings that I have termed "Core Connections." I will cover the touchy subject of faith and discuss its impact on core connections, both good and bad. I will provide one last solution that will introduce the idea of transformation and then wrap up the chapter with one final true story.

So, what is the basis for this book? What gives it credibility? Is it just a collection of nice ideas, or is there some depth underneath? In chapters one and two I introduced a philosophy and then used analogies. The philosophy was that of using nature to explain life. Is that a credible approach? In fact, there is such a thing as *order* in nature. It is specific enough to use as a foundation for thought, for reason and for a guide. Nature is even reliable enough to suggest law. We can find laws of nature in the past used to build nations. But could it be given the highest rank of a supreme authority? To answer that question, we can find one significant example. Here are the words, and you can determine if it sounds familiar:

> When, in the course of human events, it becomes necessary for one people to dissolve the political bands which have connected them with another, and to assume among the powers of the earth, the separate and equal station to which the laws of nature and of nature's God entitle them, a decent respect to the opinions of mankind requires that they should declare the causes which impel them to the separation.[76]

Yes, you probably guessed it. This is the very first paragraph of the Declaration of Independence. What authority did the founders point to that would entitle them to create a new government on this earth? The authority of the "laws of nature and of nature's God." Not only does natural law have a history of being used as an authority, it was the go-to source of authority for which to build a new nation, the United States of America. So, what about this natural law? Was it the cultural buzz of the day or was it time-tested, truly reliable, and absolute? Let's look a little closer and see if we can find some depth in this approach.

Does anybody remember the Pythagorean Theorem from high school or college math classes? The word "Pythagorean" has its roots from a group of people who lived 2,500 years ago in Greece. The Pythagoreans believed the universe conducts itself in an orderly fashion. They believed that the universe is ordered to the point of being mathematical. Thus, the Pythagorean

Theorem was born. It was a demonstration of quantifiable order.

We can quickly see that the idea of nature having order has been around a long time. Eventually the thought grew with other Greek philosophers such as Socrates, Plato, and Aristotle. By the time Aristotle had written some of his final documents the idea of God and nature was clearly evident. Aristotle's writings included: *Prior Analytics, Physics, Mechanics, On the Heavens, Reproduction of Animals, On the Soul, Metaphysics, Nichomachean Ethics, and Politics.* Wow! What a diverse set of interests. His work became a foundation of thought through the late Middle Ages right into the seventeenth century and had a strong influence in Western civilization. We need to look closer at his writings to see the brilliance of his mind. A lot of ideas were being presented at one time. Here is a sample of his writing:

> All causes at last go back to the First Cause Uncaused, all motions to the Prime Mover Unmoved; we must assume some origin or beginning for the motion and power in the world, and this source is God. God is the sum and source of all motion, so he is the sum and goal of all purposes in nature; he is the Final, as well as the First Cause.... As the tree is drawn by its inherent nature, power, and purposes toward the light, so the world is drawn by its inherent nature, power and purposes, which are God. [77]

Aristotle continues the thought that nature is available to teach us about life just as we saw with the Pythagoreans, but now he has clearly articulated an origin to that nature and introduces God into the philosophical thought.

Now, I realize it is dangerous to summarize 2,500 years in such a short manner, but my intent is to demonstrate that nature's law is a time-tested approach.

As we move into the founding era of our nation, it would be important to pay tribute to a man who had great influence in government thought to the founders themselves. His name was Sir William Blackstone. He was born in Britain and became an Oxford professor. Blackstone was the person who polished and refined nature's law into great writings that were published in Philadelphia in 1771. His place in history came at a most influential time for the budding of a new nation. His thought and approach to jurisprudence was not only the basis for many of our founders' views but also for many of our early lawyers and judges for decades to come. Blackstone's definition of natural law was this:

> This law of nature, being coeval with mankind and dictated by God himself, is of course superior in obligation to any other. It is binding over all the globe, and all countries, and at all times: no human laws are of any validity if contrary to this; and such of them as are valid derive all their force, and all their authority, mediately or immediately from this original.[78]

The authors of the Declaration shared this philosophy and pointed to the "laws of nature and of nature's God" as the foundational thought for entitling the United States of America to become a new nation. As it turns out, it is likely America's most basic core value. Today we have to be careful to maintain those core values and not build on fractured bedrock. I heard one of our top national leaders say recently that Medicare is one of our nation's core values. To me that is like saying government is one of government's core values. I don't think so.

Root Model

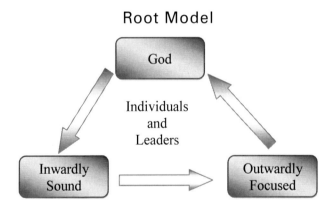

If we combine the foundational thought of God with everything from the previous chapters and summarize the research, empirical data, anecdotal stories and individual assertions, we arrive at a model that I believe dwells deep beneath the surface of right seeking individuals and leaders. At first glance it will appear oversimplified. But as we look closer beneath the surface we find the depth needed to transform a culture. Here is the transformational "Root Model":

Overview

I believe that if enough individuals and leaders possess these three core tenets within a nation, they will transform the culture of that nation.

The first tenet of the Root Model is God. As we consider Aristotle's writings, mentioned earlier in this chapter, we should place God as the "Final" and the "First." Let's see if his philosophy has any real application to our nation and our historical leaders. Let's look for the evidence. I have selected a leader from each of the last three centuries and included them in the table below:

CENTURY	LEADER	EVIDENCE OF A GOD INFLUENCE
1700s	George Washington	*George Washington's Sacred Fire* (Author: Peter A. Lillback)
1800s	Abraham Lincoln	*Abraham Lincoln A Man of Faith and Courage* (Author: Joe Wheeler)
1900s	Dr. Martin Luther King, Jr.	Dr. King was a third generation Baptist minister.

These pivotal leaders at turning points in our nation certainly had a God influence. This confirms the relevancy of Aristotle's writings to the Root Model. The second tenet of the Root Model is being inwardly sound. The third tenet is the concept of being outwardly focused. The latter two tenets have been discussed throughout the book with detailed evidence. The structure of the model however, is something new. It is positioned in a circular fashion to indicate that individuals and leaders can perpetuate themselves by following the continuum.

Now let's go for a test run and see if any of the three tenets are consistent with other well-known science or philosophy. For this purpose let's pull Maslow's Needs

Hierarchy off the shelf and position it as an example of the inwardly sound tenet. As you may remember, Maslow's hierarchy prescribes that we all start with physiological needs at the bottom of the triangle and as we progress up the triangle we end with self-actualization as the top and final need. We could easily argue that one outcome of succeeding in all of Maslow's levels within the triangle would result in an inwardly sound person. As a single tenet, Maslow can easily find a home inside the Root Model. However, from a bigger picture, there is another question to be asked: Is that where it ends?

Here is a related story. At the writing of this book, I am pursuing an MBA at Augsburg College in Rochester, Minnesota. During a recent class in organizational behavior, our professor Dr. David Conrad, Ed.D., briefly touched on Maslow's Hierarchy of Needs. When we finished the brief overview, Dr. Conrad posed a question to the class: "What is wrong with this model?" The class was quiet. I listened closely for the answer. He answered his own question "It's all about *me* .... There's got to be something *more!*" He was saying the hierarchy cannot end there; it has to lead to something outward. I was thrilled to hear an unsolicited teaching about this philosophy. I could not agree more.

Here is the problem with being inwardly sound by itself. How do we know for sure what is really going on inside the individual or leader? Until that individual does something on the outside, do we truly know what is on the inside? The proof is in the pudding. I believe an inwardly sound person will exemplify a pure heart on the inside by what they do or give on the outside. An inwardly sound person will have a propensity to give and an inwardly sound person who is mature in their soundness will want to give the best.

What is the best example of this relationship? The most telling example is selfless service. My mind immediately goes to our military. The outward focus reflects the inwardly sound nature. If there is a disciplined or pure heart on the inside, the outward act will eventually grow to be of a selfless nature. In other words, what can I do to help someone else without anything in return? This is a tough task indeed. Selfless acts are at the highest level of being outwardly focused. In the case of the military, months of self-discipline and training have grown that inwardly sound nature.

Maybe there is another side to this discussion that should be mentioned. I have heard at least two well-respected speakers state that everyone needs a payback in order for a supposed selfless act to occur. In other words, people are only motivated by getting something for themselves. Rather than challenge these well-respected leaders, I will state my response in this book. By the time each of us had reached the age of one day old, we had all created tremendous pain for our mother and a big medical bill for our mother and father, yet our parents still opted to bring this expensive pain home from the hospital. Any logical thinking human being would strike a deal with the hospital to keep the little bundle. Instead of bargaining for a better deal, our parents brought us home with excitement, a selfless act indeed.

Another example of a selfless act is the donation of a kidney or bone marrow. Not much is received in return except a lot of pain. Yet this type of selfless act occurs every day.

What happens when we release pure hearts with selfless acts into a society? These individuals influence the culture. These individuals become leaders the right way. The individuals and resulting leaders can influence a nation. These people can transform America through an inwardly sound and outwardly focused culture.

I will concede the argument made above does have some merit. Too often today the trend is going the wrong way. The individual appears to be outwardly focused but they are not inwardly sound. Their outward focus is for personal gain and not for altruistic purposes. This demonstrates we have more work to do to fully understand the dynamics of the Root Model. This provides a good introduction to a pinnacle of the book. I have termed it the "core connection."

Core Connection

The core connection is the relationship between the inward core tenet (inwardly sound) and the outward core tenet (outwardly focused) of the Root Model. This new revelation is the most significant influence on root issues I can find in years of researching this topic: the specific relationship between the inward and outward core tenets. This is at the heart of a good or bad politician. This is at the heart of a good or bad corporate leader. This is at the heart of good or bad parents.

These findings started with the terminology and discussion of Tim Spiker in Who* Not What presented in chapter eight. As I consider the issues facing our nation today, I believe there are three types of core connections found at the very heart of our society. They are destructive core connections, disharmonious core connections and constructive core connections. Let's examine each one.

Destructive Core Connections

This type of relationship is where the inward tenet and outward tenet are in harmony but result in destruction. This connection is unique in that individuals and/or leaders have incorrectly convinced themselves they are inwardly sound in an area that needs correction. Often religion will be the conduit that creates the tremendous loyalty between the two tenets in this type of connection. The most notable example is Al-Qaeda. The strategy of Al-Qaeda leaders is to use a form of their religion to convince impressionable young people that being inwardly sound includes a radical form of their religion. When the radical nature is manifested outwardly, it is a destructive core connection. The two tenets are in harmony with each other but for destructive purposes.

You may also bring to mind any number of cults that have existed in the United States that would also fall into this core connection.

A very mild form of destructive core connection is an individual who is grumpy on the inside and grumpy on the outside. This merely creates some adversity to the environment around them but still can be destructive. The only strength that I can see in the mildest form of destructive core connections is that at least the person is genuine. What you see is what you get. There are times when I might accept working with a genuinely grumpy person because at least I know whom I am dealing with.

The most common examples seen in our society today were covered in the three case studies from this book. Case study number one demonstrated that emotional abuse as a child can cause emotional eating as an adult which often leads to obesity. Something wrong on the inside causes someone to do something wrong on the outside. The inward and outward core tenets of the root model are in harmony but for destructive purposes.

Case studies two and three demonstrated that not enough time or too much trauma early in life can cause too much trouble later in life which often leads to crime. Again, something wrong on the inside causes someone to do something wrong on the outside. The inward and outward core tenets of the root model are in harmony but for destructive purposes.

Disharmonious Core Connections
This is the type of relationship that drives people nuts. For example what you are hearing on the outside of a leader sounds good but something tells you to beware of the inside. You are not really sure whom or what you are dealing with in the individual or leader. This type

of core connection is the hardest to detect of the three. As the name describes, this relationship lacks harmony between the inward tenet and the outward tenet.

The most common disharmonious core connection was presented in chapter six of this book. It is the political arena. As a matter of fact, I would say this core connection has become part of the political culture in the United States. There are actually two types of disharmonious core connections. Here is the first. The political leader is good on the inside. They genuinely love their job and want to do what is best. However, the campaign culture of rhetoric and mudslinging causes the leader to falter on the outside. In the political leader's mind, they have been forced into their actions. In other words, the end justifies the means. The result is confusion or even deception. This is the first type of a disharmonious core connection.

The second type is when the opposite occurs. The political leader is bad on the inside and yet on the outside tells you everything is good. In other words, there is a snake under the woodpile someplace. What you see on the outside does not represent what is actually happening on the inside of the individual. The more intense examples of this eventually can get discovered and end up in the headlines. You can probably think of a few political figures right now without naming names. The craftier political leaders may live a happy and seemingly healthy political life with little negative exposure. Perhaps only those who have traveled the campaign trail will see and experience the truth. Either way, the result is confusion or even deception.

Constructive Core Connections

This type of relationship is where the inward core tenet and outward core tenet of the root model are in harmony and result in a positive constructive outcome. Like the first core connection, the constructive core connection can include religion. In this connection religion is obviously used as a constructive means that benefits society as a whole either short or long term. The influence of religion will have a positive influence of good moral character on the inside and encourage the individual to act on that morality in a more altruistic manner on the outside.

The most notable examples are George Washington, Abraham Lincoln and Martin Luther King, Jr. All three of these great American leaders would fall into this category of core connections. Certainly there may have been times when they fell short, but when big decisions were on the line, this core connection generally prevailed.

The most common examples of constructive core connections come from three areas of this book. They are referenced in chapter eight with our military leaders. Second they are referenced in chapter nine with our non-profit leaders. And the third example is the average person on the street who does small leadership acts every day that receive little attention. In just a bit I will close the book focusing on you as part of this third example. I will then end the chapter with a story of a small everyday leader who has a constructive core connection.

True leaders have the inside and outside core tenets in harmony, resulting in the short or long-term good of others. This creates the long-sought-after trait in leaders called authenticity. Kevin Cashman, in his best-selling book, *Leadership from the Inside Out*, states that authenticity may be the most important and yet most challenging trait of a leader.[79]

Finally, I would point out to you that in the constructive core connection, all three core tenets are in harmony with each other: God, inwardly sound and outwardly focused.

So let me ask you a question? What kind of core connections have you experienced in your life? Personally, I think I have experienced all three. In the early years of my life I experienced a lot of destructive core connections. As I moved into my career I experienced a lot of disharmonious core connections. It is now my desire to increase my constructive core connection. My hope is for the constructive core connection to be the dominant core connection in my life.

Action

Now that we have arrived at the Root Model and the constructive core connection, how do we use this information to help society? I have provided root solutions in other chapters, but now I will focus on action that can change the negative trends in society or create a transformation in our culture. It will come through an intentional use of the Root Model and the constructive core connection. I will provide you with a step-by-step plan to accomplish this endeavor.

It is at this point in the chapter where I will start to share more of my personal opinion and reflections of root issues in America. It is at this point in the chapter where I will start to use faith as part of my last solution. In chapter nine I provided top down secular root solutions. My last solution I am about to show you will not only use faith but it will also be from the bottom up in nature. It is my intent to fully disclose this shift so that your trust will be maintained throughout the book.

In the last solution I will use the Christian faith as it is still the dominant religion in the United States and the only faith I am personally qualified to discuss.

If you have little or no interest in this last solution, you are certainly free to skip ahead. However, I would challenge you to press on and discover the way to a true root solution in your own life. Change in the world, national government, state government, local communities and families cannot happen without a change within ourselves. Join me as we finish this journey together and then wrap it up with a fictional epilogue. This epilogue will give us a look at what our America could evolve into if it keeps heading in its current direction.

Transformation

This brings us to the most important part of the book. This is where I am looking straight at you.

Here is why. Over the span of five years I have done a lot of research on root issues related to our nation and have provided some good ideas in this book up to this point. But, it is my strong belief and opinion that it is not enough. There are two reasons. First, as I mentioned, those solutions by themselves are generally top-down solutions. I genuinely feel in addition that it will take a bottom-up approach. There will need to be more. You and I will have to be involved as well. I really believe this to be true. Secondly, I feel the solutions presented in chapter nine by themselves are unsustainable without a change in our nation's culture. My experience with the U.S. State Department and the U.S. Agency for International Development tells me that sustainability is the main checkpoint for ideas related to building a nation. Therefore, the last solution in this book will need to include a sustainable transformational change in our culture. So after some reflection I could not end the book here. It would be missing the mark and falling short of the full impact of what our nation needs.

The last solution will not be a surface solution. Consistent with the rest of the book, I will focus on a root solution. I am going to introduce the idea of transformation. The last and most important solution will be transformation at the grass "root" level. I will start with you first, and then I will focus on others in our sphere of influence.

Before we discuss personal transformation we need to determine if transformation is a viable approach.

Transformational leadership is one of the most widely recognized applications of transformation. Both the academic and corporate business sectors teach or use transformational leadership, and it is even taking a front seat in leadership research. Peter Northouse, in his book *Leadership Theory and Practice,* summarizes the trends of transformational leadership this way:

> In a content analysis of articles published in *Leadership Quarterly*, Lowe and Gardner (2001) found that one third of the research was about transformational or charismatic leadership. Clearly many scholars are studying trans-

formational leadership, and it occupies a central place in leadership research.[80]

So, how does this transformational leadership relate to personal transformation? Cashman (2008) in *Leadership from the Inside Out* says the purpose of transformation is to "radiate your gifts in the service of others."[81] If we radiate these gifts in the service of others personally, we are then better equipped as leaders to help others do the same. Northouse describes this as a process whereby "a person engages with others and creates a connection that raises the level of motivation and morality in both the leader and the follower."[82] Interesting to note that being outwardly focused results in a benefit to both the recipient and the provider.

A common trait of transformation identified by Northouse is morality. Other scholars also include morality in defining transformational leadership. Krietner and Kinicki in their book *Organizational Behavior* take it even a step further and describe the transformational leader as a "moral agent":

> Transformational leaders engender trust, seek to develop leadership in others, exhibit self-sacrifice and serve as moral agents, focusing themselves and followers on objectives that transcend the more immediate needs of the work group.[83]

Wow! This is good stuff. However the definitions generally stop short of identifying the source of morality.

Sources of morality can easily be determined by studying the quotes from our founding fathers. They did not seem to be nervous or shy about articulating the source of morality. In many quotes of the founders, morality and religion was generally synonymous. Evidence can be seen in quotes from our first two presidents. During his farewell speech President Washington stated: "Of all the dispositions and habits which lead to political prosperity, religion and morality are indispensable supports."[84] Later President Adams said, "Our Constitution was made only for a moral and religious people."[85] Interesting to note here is both of these quotes not only tie faith to morality, they also seem to tie faith to sustainability. We may be on to something. The founders were not necessarily mandating religion. They were, among other things, likely imploring those who were not religious to appreciate the virtue of sustainability that faith and what it offers a nation. Atheists can benefit from the virtue of faith. They benefit from the sustainability of a nation and yet need not subscribe to any particular form of religion. At the same time those who subscribe to a faith have the freedom to do so. It can be a win-win scenario; however, we should all agree on the value and virtue of faith as it relates to sustainability.

But wait, perhaps these two quotes were isolated from the mainstream of thought from other founders of this nation. There are actually hundreds of quotes from founders related to faith.[86] Here are three more related to the sustainability of our nation:

> Religion and good morals are the only solid foundation of public liberty and happiness … While the people are virtuous, they cannot be subdued; but when once they lose their virtue, they will be ready to surrender their liberties to the first external or internal invader.[87]

> —Samuel Adams,
> signer of the Declaration of Independence

Without morals a republic cannot subsist any length of time; they therefore who are decrying the Christian religion whose morality is so sublime and pure … are undermining the solid foundation of morals, the best security for the duration of free governments.[88]

—Charles Carroll,
signer of the Declaration of Independence

The great pillars of all government and of social life: I mean virtue, morality and religion. This is the armor, my friend, and this alone, that renders us invincible.[89]

—Patrick Henry

It all comes down to two basic approaches: voluntary morality or enforced rules. Which is more sustainable? As I stated in chapter three, "If there is a daddy in every doorway, you do not need a cop on every corner." Let's look at a couple more examples of faith influencing sustainability. One of the most notable examples of using faith and sustainability in our nation is with the U.S. Military. This precedent has been used for centuries. Military chaplains date back to the Revolutionary War and still play a major role in the sustaining of individuals today. I have included pictures of faith in a war zone I personally witnessed on a regular basis.

Chaplain Dennis facilitates Bible study and prayer before the end of another day at Forward Operating Base Kalsu.

Civilians and soldiers spend time in prayer before a mission leaving from Forward Operating Base Kalsu.

Prayer before a meal by an individual soldier at Forward Operating Base Kalsu.

A second demonstration of faith influencing sustainability can be seen in the non-profit sector. One example is The Salvation Army dating back to 1879. They have impacted three different centuries by caring for those in need. The Salvation Army is motivated by faith as identified in its mission statement: "Its ministry is motivated by the love of God."[90]

Here is the result of a nation whose motto is "In God We Trust": the longest ongoing constitutional republic in the history of the world.[91] Faith absolutely affects sustainability in America. We can disagree about whether the founders were deists, evangelicals, or even atheists. What we most certainly need to agree upon is the influence of faith on the sustainability of our land. If I were atheist, I would want to know what relevance faith has to our nation today. What does faith bring to the table? Faith has influenced sustainability in the past and faith will influence sustainability in the future.

What about that political prosperity George Washington referenced well over 200 years ago? If money is your measurement of prosperity, consider the GNI (Gross National Income) of the U.S. compared to other individual nations. At the writing of this book, the GNI of the U.S. was over $14.2 trillion.[92] The next closest individual nations are less than half that amount! China and Japan are virtually tied for the number two spot at about 5 trillion each. Not only has America sustained, America has sustained with great prosperity. Washington identified the secret as religion and morality. He even went on to say that anyone who tries to remove the two (religion and morality) is not fit to be called a patriot.[93] Ouch.

Therefore, I will take a risk and talk about faith in this book as well. I will not only include the idea of faith but use the Christian faith to develop the last and sustaining solution of the book. I remember my sociology professor telling me thirty years ago that faith is part of the deepest level of our social being. Today we seem to be more tentative as a society regarding the subject. However, since I do not have a special interest group, upcoming election or political party to worry about, here we go!

Personal Transformation

Now that we have demonstrated the viability of transformation, let's go back to the Root Model and apply the model to personal transformation. What I am about to show you should look familiar. My focus is on the aspect of being intentional about these virtues inside the root model. Often, when a business is dropping down the backside of its growth curve, the owners need to reflect on what core values made them great, then dust them off and apply them in a new way to the current age. That is what we will do.

We will actually start your transformation journey in the middle of the Root Model with the core tenet of outwardly focused.

Outwardly Focused

Think of the three most outwardly focused people you know. Watch for the outwardly focused actions they do around them. Pick one action that you do not currently do, but could see yourself doing. Then do it. Let me give you an example. I have a friend named Brad who is very outwardly focused. He is a former volunteer fireman and is always helping others. My wife Jeanne and I were leaving a funeral when we ran into Brad's wife, Kari, in the lobby of the church. We asked Kari, "Where is Brad?" She pointed at the rain and cold air outside and explained that Brad went out to bring the car up to the front door of the church. Ok. Here it is. This was my teachable moment. That type of outward act is something I often forget to do and regretfully many times do not even consider. So here is my chance to be a little more outwardly focused today then I was yesterday. Out I went into the rain on a 40-degree day to get the car. When I pulled up to the church, my family members eventually came out and hopped in the car, and we drove away.. No one said anything about my small effort, but that was not the point. I was on my way to establishing a new habit that was not benefiting me.

Or was it? Something was happening way down in the deepest part of my being, and it felt good. You may be feeling good right now that I got the car for my family. In fact, it is almost assured the next time you do that outwardly focused act, the same good feeling will occur deep inside you. So, is that a cultural feeling that we experience in the west? As far as I can tell, individuals in every country I have visited or worked in experience the same good feeling. So, where does that come from? Some would argue that it is a chemical reaction in your body. Fine, but where did the idea of good come from? Who or what is the original author? I would submit to you this very good feeling is evidence of the next core tenet around the Root Model.

God

From a secular perspective this tenet would be easy to skip over or just not include in the model. However, if we thoroughly study Washington, Lincoln and King, we would not be very good researchers if we left out the significant role God played in these examples of good leaders. So, we will not dodge this part of the model but include it and explain it. If you are an atheist, you are in the right place. I will attempt to approach this subject in the same pragmatic fashion. So, with that in mind, let's consider the idea of God and the written evidence.

Three of the eight major religions of the world consider the first five books of the Bible to be inspired by

God in their original form. The very first book is called Genesis, where God is the creator of everything. I would like to point out some very specific wording that will delineate the creation of human beings along with our unique human nature. This wording I am referring to in Genesis says "according to its kind." These words are first used in reference to the creation of animals. The Bible says animals, birds and cattle were all made "according to its kind." Watch what happens when God creates man. This new creation is no longer made "according to its kind." Instead man is made "according to Our likeness."

> Then God said, "let the earth bring forth the living creature according to its kind: cattle and creeping thing and beast of the earth, each according to its kind"; and it was so. And God made the beast of the earth according to its kind, cattle according to its kind, and everything that creeps on the earth according to its kind. And God saw that it was good. Then God said "Let Us make man in Our image, according to Our likeness;"[94]

This new creation called man and woman is now made in the likeness of God. This is the very first and fundamental character we learn about you and me and our personal natures. So, if we are made like God, we need to find out who God is in His character and nature so we can learn more about who we are in our character and nature, or at least who we were originally made to be.

So, then who is God? The Bible says God is love; God is a God of order; God is gracious, giving, merciful and full of compassion, just to name a few. I would suggest to you, when we have that good feeling during that moment of loving someone else, that good feeling is a reminder of our origin. God is love; and since we are made in His likeness, we are merely exercising our "God-likeness." When you feel good during the moment of showing mercy to someone else, that is a reminder of our origin. When you feel good during that moment of giving to others, that good feeling is a reminder of our origin. It would almost be a lie to deny that the good feeling exists. As a matter of fact, it is so undeniable, we even feel good when we simply see someone else participate in an act of love and compassion. Have you ever seen a chick flick? You watch them to experience a form of love and compassion. As we discover more about our origin, we discover more about who we were intended to be as a person. As we discover more about who we were intended to be, we have more capacity to experience the next section of the Root Model.

Inwardly Sound

There are three steps to become more inwardly sound. The first step is *recognizing the source of our self-image*. Do you feel good about yourself? Who told you to feel good about yourself? My experience working with hundreds of at-risk kids tells me that our self-image comes from our biological father. They were all desperate for

THE SUMMARY AND THE TRANSFORMATION

their identity. If they felt they did not have one from a biological father, they would find an identity elsewhere.

When we get that great report card from school, it is vital that our dad sees it. Why? He is the one who forms that positive self image. Conversely, if we have a dysfunctional father, he will be the one who forms that negative self-image. Either way it comes from the father. I have found those children with a biological father in agreement with the Heavenly Father are generally blessed children. What we must understand before we move any farther is that our self-image from our biological father is only temporary. We must understand that our ultimate and final self-image comes from our Heavenly Father. It is even available to us right now. This is evidenced in the first chapter of Genesis. "God made man in His image, in the image of God He made him."[95] We might even say that we do not really know who we are until we have seen ourselves through the eyes of God. So, the first step of being inwardly sound is knowing the source of our self-image.

Transformational scholars also support the importance of self-image or identity. According to Kreitner and Kinicki, leaders can "accomplish transformation by appealing to the followers' self-concepts – namely their values and personal identity."[96]

The second step to becoming more inwardly sound is *getting rid of the things that were not meant to be part of our lives.* How do we know what to get rid of or turn away from? If we are made in the likeness of God we simply look through the Bible for the things that are not the character and nature of God. God is not hateful. He is not a God of disorder. He is not proud. As a matter of fact, he cannot have anything to do with those traits. So if we possess those traits we must turn from them. For example, when I returned home from a year in Iraq I was quick-tempered. The Bible says God is slow to anger. If we are quick tempered then we need to figure out why and get rid of it. I had to get some things cleaned up and dusted off on the inside. My emotions were running a little too thin. I had to ask myself: what is the original entry point of the temper? Eventually I found a psychologist who had experience in assisting people who returned from a war zone. The psychologist identified items in my life prior to Iraq as the entry points. Iraq was just serving to exacerbate the situation. Now I am certainly not suggesting this is the case for others returning from a war zone. I am only saying this was the situation for me.

Next, I used the Bible to clean out those areas that were unresolved before Iraq. The resolution was more forgiveness and letting go of the things that were holding me down from my past. Are there some areas of your life that need a little cleaning? Is it time to dig into those root issues you have been avoiding in your life? It may be painful to walk through, but it is vital you get a clear vision of who you are at the core. Crud from the past only seems to cloud our true self. Are you in a position to take a leadership role in resolving an unresolved matter from your past? Perhaps today is the day you sit down and write a letter to someone. Perhaps today is the day you humble yourself in order to allow resolution. Maybe you do not like to write. Maybe you can just turn and talk, just talk to God directly. But wait a minute. Would that not be an act of weakness? The Bible says, "Humble yourselves in the sight of the Lord, and He will lift you up."[97] In other words, your humility actually results in strength at the end of the day.

I can testify personally to the idea of humility. I spent my first thirty years messing up my life. It seems I have been spending my time since then trying to clean up those messes. I can say, firsthand, the humility thing works. I have spent a lot of time asking people for forgiveness. No one has turned me down yet. And today I am totally at peace with myself on the inside. It took awhile but it is worth it. You see, I know what it is like to live life without being inwardly sound. I am not saying I have arrived and am totally inwardly sound today. I am only saying I am at peace within myself, and that can be a good start. A key turning point for me was reading Proverbs from the Old Testament of the Bible. This is an objective source of truth written by King Solomon thousands of years ago. Proverbs offered me a measuring stick by which I could evaluate whether or not what I was doing was right. I found out I had some work to do. Luckily I discovered that we have a God who is patient. Yet I was empowered to not delay another day. I would encourage you to take action today with the second step of becoming inwardly sound.

The third step of becoming more inwardly sound is *strengthening the areas that were meant to be part of your life.* How do we know the areas that should be part of our life? How can we identify those traits? Study the Author, the Creator, the Maker, the One who made us in His likeness. What is His character and nature? Fortunately the Bible lists many character traits for us to pick from to emulate in our own lives: love, mercy, compassion, wisdom, humility, just to name a few. The good news is all these areas are not copyright protected or patent protected by the Creator. They are all heavenly domain and free to the public.

This may be a good time for us to go on a field trip. Personally, I learn a lot more on field trips than sitting in classrooms, no offense to those in education. I am more of a kinesthetic learner. For the field trip we will use the Christian Bible. As I mentioned earlier, Christianity is still the dominant religion in the United States and the one I am most familiar with for this purpose. I would encourage you to find a good Bible and look for the original traits of God. What is His character and nature? It works best if you can find a Bible with a concordance in the back so you can look up the trait you are seeking and find some individual spots in the Bible that you can reference. I will select two traits to get you started. If you want to read about the trait of Godly love, go to the book of 1 Corinthians and read chapter thirteen. This book is in the New Testament or towards the back of the Bible. If you would like to find a verse confirming that God is gentle go to Matthew, chapter 11, verse 29, or a more common format is Matthew 11:29. As you read these verses it should give us more information about who we should be at the core if we were made in His likeness. How do I know this will work? The Bible promises that if we seek the Lord we will find Him. It also says, "But seek first the kingdom of God and His righteousness, and all these things shall be added to you."[98] Start with one trait or character and just focus on that one before moving on to another. God is a patient God.

Let's summarize the three steps of becoming more inwardly sound. We first acknowledge the right source of our self image. Second, we turn away from the crud in our lives, thereby removing the obstacles for growth. Third, we grow and strengthen those traits we were designed to possess. Now we are on our way to becoming more inwardly sound. The good news about being more inwardly sound is the capacity to propel ourselves to the tenet of being outwardly focused again with even more capacity. The more times we travel around the Root Model, the stronger we get on the inside and the more effective we can become on the outside.

Now that we have used the Root Model for personal transformation, how can we begin to use it to transform America? Bold as it may sound, I will show you. But first we should check our assumptions again. Are "turning" and "seeking" good tactics for transforming a nation? I will answer that with a story. A couple of years ago, I was asked by our church to teach a class on the topic of God and America. I accepted and while teaching the class, an older gentleman raised his hand in the back of the class. His name was Dave and he was approaching 80. Nearly every time I called on him he would end his comment by quoting the same verse in the Bible. We knew what he was going to say before he said it. I think Dave realized we will commit something to memory if we hear it seven times. He was just trying to reach the seven mark. Well, it worked. He was passionate about his country and passionate about his faith. The verse he recited each time was, "If My people who are called by My name will humble themselves, and pray and seek My face, and turn from their wicked ways, then I will hear from heaven, and will forgive their sin and heal their land."[99] As I write this entry in the book, I am reminded of Dave as I will be attending his funeral in two days. Dave was constantly reminding us of the tactics to transforming a nation. Turning and seeking are certainly two of them.

We do have the ability to transform a nation. We need to start walking with more confidence. It will require transforming not only ourselves but individuals in our personal sphere of influence, people you are close to in life. It will be easier than you think.

Transformation of Others

The next step after revolving around the Root Model yourself is to do it again. This time take someone with you. This point is pivotal in the book. Here we transition to real action, your action. It is simple and something everyone can do. You will not be responsible for the nation, but you will take some responsibility for your sphere of influence. Are you ready? I am asking you to try this for one month and then step back and evaluate if your intentional effort generated a sense of influence. Here is what I am asking you to do. Go around the Root Model with a teenager or someone who is younger. This is how we begin to transform the nation. Let me show you just how easy it can be. Here in Minnesota we have something called "Minnesota nice." Generally it means we try to be nice to others when we are out in our daily routine (driving in heavy traffic is exempt, apparently).

One of the growing examples of Minnesota nice is something called the drive-through difference. It simply means paying the bill for the person behind you at the drive-up window of a restaurant. I will admit, I have only done it a few times in my life. However, one time my family was in the car with me. Our adult children were in the back seat, and they were very engaged as I went through the process. We were all a little anxious about the whole thing, and my family was looking back for any reaction from the recipient and then quickly looking away. They were laughing and making comments and even discussing the experience on our way down the road after leaving the restaurant. The outcome was a positive experience for everyone involved. The person behind us still had the option of paying for his own meal, but I am guessing most people receive the gift. Some even repeat the favor and pay for the people behind them. Now, how much time and effort did that take? Very little, I did not even get out of my seat to put this act in motion. However, it did have influence on the next generation of our society in some small way. Hopefully, you are starting to think about the times when you have had similar experiences, experiences where you helped someone else. The other person may or may not have been soliciting your help. What I am asking of you today is to be more intentional about these acts. Set a goal of three outwardly focused acts in the next month. Can you do it? Think about those young people around you that you have been intending to spend a little time with. Or maybe you have children around you in your immediate family. That is the place to start.

How important is this? This very act you are about to do is what feeds all the other ideas in this book. It fuels the solutions in chapter nine. It is what lays the foundation for true transformation. It is at the core of the root issues we have discussed. Walking the next generation through any of the tenets of the Root Model brings forth the same attributes of Washington, Lincoln and King. Raising up an inwardly sound and outwardly focused young person will provide the hope for our nation. It will more fully equip a future father. It will more fully equip a future mother. It will help create a genuine leader. It will provide the local leaders needed in our community. It will provide more genuine leaders in the business sector. It will provide more genuine leaders in the non-profit sector. It will provide a contingency of people who are truly equipped to lead our nation with authenticity, leaders who will be positive role models for the generation after them. As adults in this country we will pass on those three tenets of leadership or we will let them fall through the cracks, leaving the next generation ill-equipped to face future adversity.

My hope is that you will want to continue moving around the model in subsequent months and then it will become a habit and part of your character and nature. And who will benefit the most? You will. My hope is

264 | STEVEN J. WILSON

that you can have that good feeling year round and at the same time help transform our spheres of influence. Eventually it can transform our culture.

I have spent most of my life engaging with others for the sake of benefiting myself. That needs to change. It will not happen by itself. I will need to be intentional.

When I step back and analyze the simplified nature of the Root Model, I ask myself if this could really have much of an impact on society. Then I think about the Enron scandal. If the responsible parties had the Root Model engrained into their being, would it make a difference? What about the collapse of the housing market and the bad loans inside the investment banking industry? If the Root Model would have been engrained within the responsible parties, would it make a difference? What about the private business owners or executives who give themselves a 186% raise and give their average employee a 7% raise? If the Root Model was engrained within the responsible parties, would it make a difference? I think the answer in all three cases is yes.

In the solutions chapter I provided a solution for social root issues and political root issues but I did not provide a root solution for the business sector. Ironically, the business sector is where my passion lies at the moment. I am currently working with small business owners to incorporate an outwardly focused mindset while they are still small so it can become engrained in their approach as they expand and grow. How successful will my efforts be? I don't know the answer, but what I do know for sure is sitting on the sidelines is no longer an option.

Transformed businesses will lead to transformed cities. Transformed cities will lead to a transformed nation. Finally we arrive at that point in the book where we are, as the subtitle says: "transforming America with an inwardly sound and outwardly focused culture."

If you still have doubt left in your mind about the importance of the root model and the importance of transformation, I am ready for you. My daughter, Brittany, has written a fictional epilogue that will help us understand what our society can look like in 20 years if we ignore the tenets of the Root Model. The epilogue will challenge you and entertain you at the same time. You cannot end this book without reading the epilogue.

In chapter eight I shared several stories of experiences I have personally had with leaders who are inwardly sound and outwardly focused. Before moving to the fictional epilogue, I will end this chapter with one final true story.

FINAL STORY

"Well, ma'am, I have some news about your situation." The doctor was struggling with how to share this with his patient. "I am happy to tell you that you are pregnant."

That was not something new for Elrey, as this would be her fourth child. Generally families were larger in 1961.

The doctor continued. "Unfortunately, I have to also tell you that you have cervical cancer."

Elrey did not know how to respond. Can you imagine being the recipient of that news? How do you react? What a mixed message. What a diagnosis. Everything that was just said would change a person's life forever. She went home to tell her husband and then face this challenge over the next several months. A battle for life was occurring inside of her. Three things were competing for life: Elrey, the new baby, and the cancer. Maybe one or two of the competing forces would survive.

Options could be considered to preserve the life of the mother. It has been reported that even in 1961, there were 210,000 legal abortions made in such situations. In this situation, however, it was never considered. Eventually a baby boy was born full term. Elrey went back three months later and had surgery. The surgery was completely successful, and fifty years later, the baby and mother are still doing fine. The boy and mother lived, and the cancer died. This is a story I know well, as I was the baby in 1961. You see, I am the benefactor of someone else being inwardly sound and outwardly focused. Thanks, Mom. I love you!

ROOT LESSON FROM CHAPTER TEN:
Maybe God is real after all.

EPILOGUE

BY BRITTANY WILSON

INTRODUCTION

You are now entering the bonus round. You have finished reading the nonfictional side of the book, and now you are in for a treat. I would like to introduce you to my daughter, Brittany. She will entertain you with a dramatic fictional epilogue. Brittany will use her artistic talents to demonstrate the potential outcome of root issues left in the ground.

At the writing of this book, she is finishing her undergraduate degree in psychology. I have asked her to take us into the future. What could our nation look like in twenty years? What happens if we allow members of Congress to be inwardly focused? What happens if we continue to ignore the issue of fatherless homes? What happens if I ignore my responsibility to influence our culture? Brittany has crafted a fictional story that will help us experience the answers. This is by far the most dramatic part of the book! It is entertaining and thought provoking at the same time. Please remember this is where the non-fiction ends and the fictional part of the book begins.

Brittany Wilson, Epilogue Author.

2012

A notebook sat blankly on my lap as I listened to the slow hum of the radiator in the corner. I hated coming into a professor's office; however, my grade had slowly begun to drop, and I couldn't afford another "C". As the economics expert walked in, I stood up to politely greet him with a handshake and thanked him for his time.

"Okay, Melinda, what can I do for you?" he asked me as I sat down uncomfortably in the ugly orange chair. This was the fourth meeting we had had this last week, and I was getting frustratingly used to the brown eyes that peaked out from under the bush he called eyebrows. His face was clearly worn with age, and he had a strange habit of crinkling his nose when he was thinking hard. I started to think about his question. What could he do for me? He could give me a good grade. I was sick of these general classes. They were boring to me and didn't assist me at all in the pursuit of my future psychology degree.

Instead, through a soft smile I replied, "Could you please share with me the importance of the change of our governmental system?"

I grabbed a pen out of the binding of the notebook and pushed back its cover. After fingering through the countless pages of notes, my hand rested on the first blank page in anticipation of his answer. I looked up to see him staring directly at me. I redirected my gaze back to my notebook and slowly wrote down the date, "4/12/2012." I continued to outline the numbers until he began to speak.

"That's a very good question. Our current governmental system is slowly being overrun with debt. Instead of paying back the money we owe, we keep accumulating more just in interest alone. Most don't realize how much destruction awaits us if we don't fix this problem now. We are currently racking up trillions of dollars in debt and the future generations, you and your children, will pay the price."

As he spoke, I slowly doodled on the top of the paper. I had heard this speech before, and it had already gotten old. I honestly didn't care about the debt. *We have been in debt before, I'm sure. I mean, the Great Depression must have been worse than this.*

He adamantly continued. "We have had debt before, but not to this level. The projected outcome is irreversible."

I looked up at him as he strangely seemed to read my mind. His eyes were diverted to the ceiling as he leaned back in his swivel chair with his hands on his balding head. He clearly seemed at ease despite the intensity in his voice. "Everyone seems to have a theory about the solution to this growing problem."

Not me, I thought as I smiled at my own amusement. "Let the representatives take care of it; that's their job, right?"

"Well, I personally think the solution is simple; however, it is a lot more difficult to attain than it seems. It starts in the home," he confidently stated, pushing his finger into the desk and sitting up straight.

He looked straight in my direction; however, he seemed to be looking to a place beyond me. He did this at times when he was making a point. I was pretty sure I could be making a face, and he wouldn't notice. He was known for being a very astute professor, but I often wondered if he was a tad loony.

He continued his speech. "That is where a person begins. That is where people develop their values, their personality. If our current adults were taught from their parents years ago to manage their money and not spend what they don't have, everyone would be a lot better off. Are you getting this?"

He had come out of his haze and was clearly staring at my graffitied notebook. I had accidently lowered it into his line of vision, and he could clearly see the shooting star I was drawing in the margin. I quickly pulled my notebook out of his sight.

"Of course, continue," I stated with what I would like to call a charming smile. He took a deep breath as he looked at me with squinted eyes. He took a moment to milk the silence before proceeding.

"So, one may ask, what is the solution? We clearly can't force parents to teach good habits. Statistics show 40 percent of children come home from the hospital to a fatherless home. How do we change this?"

I had no idea. *People have the right to raise their children however they want, even if that includes being raised in a fatherless home, right?*

I left the professor's office that day more confused than when I entered. If the United States was so messed up, then why were we the superpower of the world? As soon as I got back to my dorm, my wandering mind forgot the worries from the meeting, and I didn't think about those worries again until twenty years later.

2032

A door is a simple object to most. It is merely an inanimate object that stands between them and their destination. So simple, in fact, that most people would not even consider the opening of a door an event to be accomplished in their day-to-day life. I, however, was different.

So there I was, my hand hovering over the door knob, my eyes attentively watching as if my hand had a brain of its own. The fight had begun in my mind, and I didn't know if I had any desire to beat it. Over the years, my hesitancy had become a way of life. I had overcome many obstacles in my life; however, this was one that lingered. I could hear the shuffle of papers and loud conversations awaiting my arrival. I chuckled at how stupid this scenario would look to any observer. I had several options. As I began listing the possible options in my mind, the door flung open, and I was stomach to stomach with my pregnant secretary. She gasped and jumped back, clenching her hand to her chest.

"Jeez, Dr. Schultz, you scared the bejeebers out of me!" she exclaimed, giggling as she pushed the blonde curls from her eyes. "What are you doing in here? You have five voicemails, Timothy on line one, and your 8 a.m. in the waiting room."

She unprofessionally linked her arm with mine as she led me out of the hallway and into the chaos. As we entered, a skeletal woman sat stiffly in one of the red, flowered chairs, anxiously wringing out her boney fingers. The morning light showered her face from the window across the room. The light accentuated the lines under her eyes, clearly too old for her face. She held a similar aura to most of the patients I spoke to on a daily basis: *desperation*. Since the IMF had taken over the national debt a few years ago, most Americans had suffered the results of the extreme budget cuts. Many of my recently added clients were non-regulars that came to me as a last resort. Her pale eyes drifted in our direction as we entered. She stood up quickly to greet me with a weak smile and an extended hand.

"Dr. Schultz, my name is Malva Hayes."

I unlinked arms with my clingy secretary and gently shook her moist hand. I cringed a little as our hands separated.

"Nice to meet you, Malva. You can come with me," I greeted her sweetly with a smile as we walked into my office. "You may shut the door behind you, my dear, and make yourself comfortable on either of the couches." I gestured to the two sofas that sat facing my desk. Strangely, I could feel myself begin to treat her like a child, despite the fact that she appeared much older than my thirty-eight years.

She sluggishly entered the room and took a look around. Each movement appeared to be slow motion. Her fingers played with the stringy red hair that surrounded her face. She sat down gently and looked at me. This woman intrigued me. I was interested to know what life had dealt her, creating such an emotionally injured spirit.

"Let's begin, Malva. What brings you in today?" I slowly took a notebook and pen from the top desk drawer, feeling my back cringe with exhaustion and trying to mirror the speed in which she moved.

"Um ... I have never been to a therapist before." Her eyes lowered back to her lap, clearly a sign of discomfort.

"Why don't we start by you telling me a little bit about *you*. And don't worry; the next hour will be over before you know it. We won't move faster than you are willing."

"Well," she began, seemingly gaining courage, "I have been married to my wife, Carol, for seventeen years. We adopted two children right after we got married. Ginger is now fifteen, and Sander is sixteen. The three of them are my life. I am a stay-at-home mom, and Carol is a professor at the university."

"Difficult ages," I replied.

"What?"

"Your children."

"Oh, yes. They are wonderful, though," she assured me as a small smile crossed her face. "They struggle at times, but who doesn't?" she said confidently, nodding her head as if to reassure herself.

"Tell me more about your children."

Her eyes rose to look out at the skyscape outside the window above the adjacent couch.

"What would you like to know?" Her eyes seemed tender at the topic, still refusing to move from the window.

"Do they still go to school?"

"Ginger does. She is just like Carol, always wanting to achieve something great." She looked at me and smiled. "Sander quit a year ago."

I nodded, genuinely listening to her words. I couldn't help but sympathize with this woman. It was clear to me that she had a full heart for the people in her life.

"Carol…tell me about her." I spoke softly to reassure Malva that she was accepted here.

"Carol is wonderful to me." She paused, and her gaze shifted back to her hands. The room got quiet for a brief moment before her eyes rose to meet mine. I waited, giving her the chance to add more. "We, uh, we met in college. We had immediate chemistry, and it has been that way ever since. Naturally, we underwent difficulty with lesbian rights, but five years later our dreams came true, and we were allowed to marry."

"How does your family get along with each other?"

I watched her eyes glaze over as she seemed to fade into a different place. Her whole body appeared to freeze as her thoughts consumed her being. Her presence in the room quickly returned as my office door was flung open and in popped the head of my disruptive secretary. My eyes darted back and forth between my quieted patient and my assistant in a sign that her presence was completely unprofessional and quite disturbing.

"I am sorry to disturb you, Dr. Schultz, but you have a visitor that has urgent business to discuss with you," my secretary rapidly informed me.

"I will be out shortly, Jackie." I calmly but sternly attempted to warn her as my eyes floated to the patient sitting across from me. Her legs were now crossed one over the other, and she was calmly looking at me, clearly out of the haze she had been in just moments ago. I was having trouble believing how awful the timing of the disturbance was.

"Uh, it's important, Dr. Schultz." Jackie had a puzzled expression on her petite face as she attempted to convey a serious situation.

"I will talk to him when I finish, my dear," I repeated, starting to wonder what possibly could cause Jackie to frantically enter my office in the middle of a counseling session. She bit her lip as she slowly began to back out the door.

"It sounds important, Dr. Schultz. Don't miss it on my account," Malva responded as her focus shifted to Jackie, who had reentered the room at her own invitation. I could not fathom how uncomfortable this moment was. I calmly agreed, assuring both parties that the visit would not last longer than a few short minutes. I swiveled my chair away from my desk and stood up calmly as did Malva.

"You stay here, my dear," I cautioned. "Make yourself comfortable, and I will be back in one moment."

Malva sat back down and allowed herself to relax into the plush sofa. I studied her as I made my way out the door. As I strode into the lobby, a man in a blue pin-striped suit was awaiting my arrival. I couldn't help but be slightly irritated at the urgency of his presence. I could feel myself reverting toward my high school days and had a sudden urge to make fun of the drastic comb-over I was sure he called hair. I talked myself out of it and looked into his plump face. "Can I help you?" I asked blandly, split between irritation and curiosity.

"Dr. Schultz, my name is Kent Warren."

Kent Warren. The name sounded vaguely familiar, but I couldn't place it. I could feel the stress rise up in my stomach from the tone in his voice. I took two breaths of air as I waited for him to continue.

"I am the personal secretary of Governor Cassidy, and it is my duty to inform you, and many other psychologists, that your workload will be doubled on account of IMF order."

My eyes did not leave his face. I was starting to learn the true meaning of speechless. I bit my inner lip as I spit out the first words that came into my mind in a storm of frustration.

"Excuse me? Sorry, *Kent*, was it?" I could feel myself get snippy as I began to defend myself and the patients already in my care. I waited for his affirmative nod, took a calming breath, and continued. "I have already had to double my load in the last few years, and my days and weekends are already booked. If I add any more patients, the adequate amount of patient care that I am able to give now will be compromised. Why would the IMF see it as the best interest of anyone to add patients to an already booked therapist?"

In recent years, the International Monetary Fund had become big news. Only a few years before, the federal government had agreed to a merger with the IMF. America had only been able to pay its debts to other nations by borrowing more money. The nation essentially went bankrupt, leaving a $27 trillion debt to the global community. The merger agreement stated that Americans could still maintain possession of their personal and corporate property; however, the IMF was ultimately in control of their money. The IMF was in control of the value of the dollar and the money stream. The IMF made all major financial decisions regarding the United States of America.

What I didn't understand was how this correlated to me and my workload.

"The IMF has issued budgetary cuts upon our prison system. There are no more funds set aside for building new prisons, so this means that we are limited to the prisons that we currently have, and they are filled. The option that is left is requiring convicted felons to do community service and sending them to counseling in hopes that it will provide a cheaper and more efficient option."

I could feel my emotions go limp. They are doubling my load with convicted felons? I was speechless. I could feel the nerves in my stomach begin to tighten. I had entered this career to help people, not to become a jail warden. I would be murdered, and there would be no consequences for the murderer, but more work for another counselor. My head began to spin. I could feel my anxiety rise up like a wave smashing into a brick wall. There was nothing I could do to get away from this situation. I couldn't quit; I would be jobless in a jobless market. I was one of the few who could still work enough to afford living. Not that the money that I was getting paid was worth anything anymore. The dollar held no monetary value outside of the United States.

After I didn't respond, the pudgy assistant attempted to lighten the mood by stating, "But everyone has to make sacrifices during this time. Everyone is contributing their piece."

He continued, but I couldn't hear him anymore. My breakfast was spinning in my stomach. I held up a finger to stop his mindless chatter and ran to the bathroom and slammed the door behind me. My entire breakfast swiftly sloshed into the toilet as I knelt, clasping the bowl between my knees. I could feel germs crawling up from the toilet, tormenting my mind as they began to inhabit my skin. My exhaustion had reached a peak, and every moment I spent sitting here made it worse. More acid traveled up my throat and out of my mouth. The burn on the back of my throat diminished. I swallowed, attempting to remove the taste from my tongue. Never would I have imagined twenty years ago that this is what would have come of my life. Never would I have imagined that I would be the one struggling with how to survive in this society.

I struggled to take a deep breath but the air quivered as I let it out. I tried again to gain the strength to stand. I had to rid myself of the stress that soaked me. Malva Hayes. Suddenly I remembered the petite woman waiting for me in my office. I had to be strong. My mind argued with my body. *Just send Malva home; who cares anymore.* Her pale eyes appeared in front of my face. So vulnerable; I had no choice but to help. I took a deep breath again and let it out smoothly. I was ready. I repressed my nerves as I grabbed the hand rail next to the toilet. I slowly lifted my body to standing and waited for my vision to clear. Another breath. As I walked to the door I resisted the urge to look in the mirror. I couldn't deal with the bags that I am sure haunted my face. As I reentered the lobby, the overweight Kent Warren was watching the birds outside the window as they flew above the city. His gaze quickly shifted to me as I walked by.

"Our business is done, Mr. Warren." I stated confidently trying to gain control of my quivering voice.

"Actually, there are a few…" I cut him off as I shut the door behind me, knowing that running from my problems was wrong, but seeing it as the only option. I had to get back to Malva, who I now saw had been waiting patiently this whole time. Unsure of how long I had been away, I greeted her gently and apologized for my absence. She, of course, said it was no problem and we proceeded with the session. As I sat across from her, I found it interesting that her demeanor had gotten more comfortable. I couldn't help but wonder if she had overheard anything that had been said in the lobby. It almost felt as if the roles had shifted and she was now the one more at ease. I tried to relax and reached for the notebook that was resting on the desk.

"Can I ask you a question, Dr. Schultz?" Malva carefully formed her words.

"Of course," I assured forcing a smile and nodding.

"Are you ok?"

I let out a low and whispered chuckle as I measured the turn this session had taken.

"Yes. Yes, of course." I assured her. "This is your time. I am so sorry I have taken up so much of it. Now you tell me, how are you?" I had gotten used to blowing off my own emotions during therapy sessions; however, today's stress was particularly difficult to ignore. I knew my face was the white of a bleached sheet, but attempted to revert the attention to her.

"I am fine." She stated nodding, still trying to analyze my face. I solidly covered my stress and worry and allowed myself to dive into this therapy mindset again. My stomach churned as it soaked up my repression with acid.

"Tell me about Sander," I said.

Her vision seemed to immediately cloud over again, clearly a touchy subject. "What would you like to know?" she asked softly. She began to wring her hands out once more and returned her gaze to the ground. I wondered if she knew how clearly she wore her expressions on her face. My intrigue with this woman came back as I began to analyze her actions and ignore my twisted stomach.

"Do you agree with his decision to quit school?"

"Well, that is typical of a child his age." I looked down at my notebook and wrote, *Calling 16 year old: child.*

"So, it doesn't bother you then?"

"No....no it doesn't bother me," She assured me, shaking her head.

"What does he do now that he is out of school?" I asked. The room got quiet as her gaze painted the floral wallpaper. It was curious to me why this question appeared difficult to answer.

"He, uh... he... well... I don't know." I waited to see if she would continue, trying to lessen the tension. "He is a great kid, Dr. Schultz." She stated making eye contact with me once more. I reassured her with a genuine nod and light smile. "We disagree a lot... when he is home." She paused to think before continuing. "He struggles, I think. He doesn't get along with Carol. And the two of them fight."

Her story was beginning to make sense of her exhausted demeanor. "What do they fight about?"

"About Candace." Candace? I searched my brain for this name, but had trouble coming up with the answer. "His daughter." My heart jumped as she answered my question quietly. I couldn't help but wonder why she hadn't mentioned Candace when I asked her about her family earlier. As I struggled with how to respond she gently continued. "She is a little less than a year old and cuter than any child I have seen before." As she spoke I could feel the burden of her words weigh more and more.

"Where is her mother?" I watched her carefully as I spoke, afraid to dig too quickly into her situation. While I was talking she pulled her small legs into her stomach and encased them with her arms. Her demeanor was built on innocence. I looked down at my notebook and quickly sketched the words "obvious regression." I returned my eyes to her as she began to answer.

"I don't know. Sander doesn't talk to us about her and the only time we have met her was in the hospital." As Malva's situation deepened my stomach began to turn with the same doubt I had on the day I met my first client. How could I help this woman when I had such tormenting problems of my own? I looked at her as she spoke. It was so weird to have such doubt about my own abilities. *I can do this*, I thought to myself. I just had to get through the day. I took another quiet breath and let my eyes shut briefly to attempt to lessen my stress. My stomach swiftly turned and screamed within me. I swallowed and continued.

"You had mentioned that Carol and Sander don't get along. How does that affect you?"

"I feel so torn. Carol and I are so happy together; we have our difficulties like every marriage, but it is great. It is really hard having them fight all the time."

"Of course it is," I reassured. "What do they fight about?"

"Carol thinks that Sander needs to move out if he isn't going to mature and start taking responsibility for his actions. He is living in this fantasy world where he can do whatever he wants whenever he wants and doesn't have to face reality. Candace was a breaking point for Carol, and she gave Sander an ultimatum to shape up or get out. I think he might leave."

"Does Candace live with you?"

"Yes." She nodded.

"Is Sander a good father?" At this question, Malva let out a low tone as she thought.

"He could be, I think." She lightly pulled at the bottom of her faded jeans as she spoke. "He just seems so lost. Searching." I nodded, knowing full well that this was a common situation among most teens. Direction was hard to give someone, especially now with the country in a state of flux.

Sudden beeping signaled the end of the meeting. I was torn between a desire to help and a need to clear my stomach once more of the toxins that raged within me. Malva looked softly at me and smiled showing her appreciation despite the interruption. I didn't want her to leave yet. Her heart seemed so tender and real, a trait I didn't see much anymore. As she stood up my heart began to hurt for her as I let myself connect with a patient for the first time. She slowly stood, retreating back to her slow motion demeanor.

"It was really nice to meet you, Dr. Schultz." Malva graciously shuffled over to me and shook my hand.

I covered our hands with another, knowing full well the consequences this would have on me later. "Anytime, Malva." I led her to the swinging door and pushed it with my shoulder, careful to not let it touch my hands. I held it open as she daintily wandered through. She turned and quickly waved as she passed through the lobby and out the door. I was strangely saddened at her absence as I stared at the door. I was very surprised at how much I had bonded with this woman over such a—

"Whatcha looking at?" I could feel the heat of the words on my ear as I turned to see my secretary one foot from my face. As her words brought me to reality, the tightness returned in my stomach. "If you are worried about forgetting to have her pay, I charged her before the session," she stated looking for affirmation. I watched her hands rub circles on her enlarged stomach, debating whether or not to affirm her or blow her off.

"Good job, Jackie." I affirmed, curious of how her innocent personality would change when her child was born.

"Timothy called this morning. I took a message and told him you would return his call. He is so sweet; you should marry him." Jackie nodded her head in agreement with herself. I grunted, knowing full well that she was aware of my view of marriage as an empty promise.

"When is my next appointment?" I asked, changing the subject.

"Five minutes!" Jackie sang as she wobbled back to her desk. I thanked her as I pushed the door open with my shoulder. "Oh and Dr. Schultz! Mr. Warren said he would return tomorrow to discuss details about the increase in patients." Her voice rang through the door as it closed behind me.

I collapsed into my chair and rested my head in the palm of my hands. I could feel the stress well up into my eyes as I began to recall all of the events of the day. My fingertips dug into the temples of my head as I tried to gain a hold of myself. It was too late. It was times like this that I wished I could cry. Instead, my stomach once again built up into a ton of bricks. I let my hands fall loosely to my desk as my gaze drifted up to the pimpled ceiling. Ironically, I had never noticed the ceiling before. Every dot was different than all the others but stuck to the same surface and destined to watch time pass it by. Just like me, helplessly living out my life according to what everyone destined for me. I couldn't help but remember the prophetic words of my professor twenty years ago warning me of the danger that lay ahead.

It was too late now. America had become a permanent slave to its own debt. The first decision by the IMF was to defund the United States military and contract the United Nations to provide security. The United States was no longer a threat or an ally to the world. It was simply a historically great nation. The social dysfunction and financial dysfunction became the rule rather than the exception. No nation ever conquered the United States. The United States conquered itself.

APPENDIX

PROCESS USED TO CREATE THE PAN-TIME THEORY CHART FROM CHAPTER FOUR

First, we will form a grid that will be used as a framework.

Input		Output			
Hours of Nurturing per Day	Crime %	Grad %	Welfare %	Employ %	Home Own %
High					
Medium					
Low					
Very Low					

This lays out a table that will allow us to look at different levels of nurturing and the projected outcomes from the time and trauma theory on a few selected social indicators.

Now let's add some data. We will use three general sources. The numbers are real and well documented; however, fitting them into this grid is totally hypothetical. This style of simulating data I will admit upfront is a bit crude. Data from different sources brought into one grid introduces all kinds of variables that may have little parallel from one study to the next. It also removes the needed control group.

Now that I have totally discredited the grids, I would like to say that my point in designing these tables is to demonstrate the tremendous impact time and trauma could have on our nation if not taken more seriously. In other words, even though the application of the numbers is hypothetical, the trends are real, and it is worthy of a closer look by those who have the money and education to take this theory to the next level of research.

Now then, the first set of numbers comes from the very well-known research of the Perry Preschool Project.[100] This is a forty-year project following at-risk youth from childhood into their middle age of life. Let's enter this first set of numbers.

Input	Output				
Hours of Nurturing per Day	Crime %	Grad %	Welfare %	Employ %	Home Own %
High (Normal)					
Medium					
Low	36	65		76	27
Very Low	55	45		62	5

The second set of numbers was published in November of 2006 by America's Promise[101] and cited research completed by Heckman and Cunha.

Input	Output				
Hours of Nurturing per Day	Crime %	Grad %	Welfare %	Employ %	Home Own %
High (Normal)		90	3	95	67
Medium	19	85			
Low			9		
Very Low			18		

BACKGROUND FOR PREDICTION ARRESTS AND PREGNANCIES

Based on the numbers and trends, my prediction is this: It is likely 25 percent of babies born today will either be arrested or have an unwanted pregnancy by age eighteen.

What supports this prediction I have italicized above? The first reason is the trend of time being spent with our youth as outlined earlier in the book. Second, if you combine 2006 information from the U.S. Census Bureau and the OJJDP[102] (Office of Juvenile Justice and Delinquency Prevention), it shows that 12.24 percent of our nation's teenagers ages fifteen to seventeen committed a crime. These were juvenile arrests for that age group just in 2006. Obviously the cumulative effect by age eighteen would be higher. Simply doubling this number alone in twenty years would project a 25 percent cumulative crime rate for eighteen year olds. This does not include unwanted pregnancy and therefore should be a conservative speculation.

SUPPORT FOR THE RISE IN TEEN PREGNANCY

What supports the idea that teen pregnancy will continue to rise? Our teenagers are growing more sexually active, as demonstrated in the next paragraph.

A CDC report in early 2008 showed that 25 percent of teen girls between the ages of fourteen and nineteen have at least one sexually transmitted disease.[103] This is astounding! Does this make anyone else want to stand up and shout, "Stop this social train, it isn't working"? The considerations grow even worse. What percent of these teenage girls will end up with cervical cancer? How many will become sterile? What societal impact occurs if these numbers continue to increase?

COST OF FATHERLESS HOMES

Crime	Estimated Annual Cost: $100 Billion

According to the National Institute of Justice,[104] the annual cost of the crime in the U.S. can be between $400 and $500 billion. Depending on which study you cite, 70-85% of offenders come from fatherless homes. One could make an initial argument that easily $225 billion could be attributed to fatherless homes, however since this is an estimation, let's use $100 billion to be safe. Fatherless homes are certainly one of the main contributors to the time and trauma issue in America.

Education	Estimated Annual Cost: ?

What is the cost of education in schools with 50% graduation rates or sub-par graduation rates at any level? In Minnesota, for example, the basic per pupil education formula rate is seemingly higher in school districts and neighborhoods with high poverty rates. Obviously the higher cost of education in these school districts across the country amounts to billions. Many of these school districts around the country are in poverty areas with high concentrations of fatherless homes.

Welfare	Estimated Annual Cost: $100 Billion

A child in a single-parent home would certainly be in the "time" category. I believe this to be self-evident. If the child were in a two-parent home, the welfare costs for single-parent programs would not occur.

The base information comes from the Heritage Foundation Article dated August 1, 2001 for the year 2000. The document showed total welfare including state and federal at a cost of $434 billion for FY 2000.[105] Of the $434 billion, 34% went to single-parent or no-parent homes.[106] We can assume that most of these children were *voluntarily* left behind by one or two parents. Some of the children may have *involuntarily* been left behind. The main example of involuntarily is the death of a parent.

If we estimate that 70% of the children in these single-parent or no-parent homes are a result of voluntary abandonment, than we can assume approximately $100 billion per year is related to time.

Employment	Estimated Annual Cost: $24 Billion

What does it cost when people are in prison and not employed? There is a loss of revenue to our society in the form of taxes. The taxes can include FICA and income taxes. Let's say that same prisoner having had the proper time as a child and little trauma would be earning $40,000 per year. The average total tax on that $40,000 can estimate approximately 40% including all federal, state and local taxes. With our prison and jail population over 2 million[107] the total cost would be $32 billion and with 75% of inmates coming from fatherless homes we can attribute approximately $24 billion of lost revenue. This loss of revenue is just from the prison population and does not consider the unemployment that time and trauma may have impacted with those outside of prison. For example, the unemployment rate is nearly 30% historically for inmates prior to arrest.[108]

Home Ownership	Estimated Annual Cost: ?

The last row on the chart is home ownership. Decreasing percent of home ownership in the future is problematic. First of all, this decreases the tax base of real estate taxes for local communities. Less taxes means slower community progress and growth. Second, decreasing percent of home ownership in the slightest degree affects construction and the number of jobs in the trade industry. Third, less home ownership means fewer services and less consumer spending for home maintenance and improvement. I will let you pick a number.

Total Estimated Cost of Just Three of the Five	Estimated Annual Cost: $224+++ Billion

OVERCOMING OBESITY;
CONTINUATION OF CHAPTER THREE
Written by Guest Contributor
Don Carlson

Not long ago I was chatting with a woman who had struggled with a weight problem. After I told her about this way of looking at her relationship with food, she told me a little about her husband. For him, food was something that he enjoyed but never felt a reason to overeat. When he had had enough, he just stopped eating. Until the next time he was hungry, he had no compulsion to go for food, yet he liked to savor a good meal as much as the rest of us. She related that he still wore the same size clothes that he had worn in high school over twenty years ago. For the folks who do not struggle with their relationship with food, they still have the same emotional needs that the rest of us do. But, for whatever reason, they are able to move on to find other ways of meeting these inner needs. As they grew up, they learned to focus their energies on developing relationships around love, intimacy, companionship, common interests, and meaningful friendships. Food does not have the meaning to them that it has to us.

Take one very serious, sober moment to ask yourself this question: How is this relationship with food working out for you? You ask food to be *comfort food*, to give you intimacy, but the best it can do is give you a momentary sugar high which, if your body is inactive, is often followed by an insulin low. You ask food to relieve your stress, but in the long term it only adds stress to your body. You want it to soothe your loneliness, but it eventually works to foster more lone-liness. You consume unnecessary amounts of food so there is something you can have control over, but in the end, food seems to have control over you.

Ponder this: Is having a relationship with food a lit-tle like having a best friend that constantly gets you in trouble? Time after time, you have done all kinds of things to make the relationship work, but you regularly end up disappointed. Maybe you need to think about bringing an end to this relationship.

To understand this new concept, you need to grasp that you are not divorcing yourself from food. If you did this, you would starve to death. Instead, you will pon-der taking the steps to end your relationship with food.

To get a handle on this, let's take a look at what it means to go through a painful separation. Some of you have already experienced a divorce from another per-son, so you will recognize this painful process. Others, who have never been married, may see aspects of sepa-ration or loss which may have occurred in your own lives. Nearly everyone has had a relationship with a boss or coworker that did not turn out the way they hoped it would. Take a look at a simple progression of how a relationship can become dysfunctional and thus move toward separation. To do this, examine the steps of that separation.

- After having lived with a given relationship for any period of time, there evolves a group of expectations about how the relationship will function. Without going through a long analy-sis of expectations, it is safe to say that when one or more of these get disappointed, there awaits an opportunity for stress and conflict. Some of this is bound to happen in any relationship. Most of the time people figure out who will do what, or how the expectation might be negotiated and changed; then life goes on. Some of these expectations are easy to talk about, and a strategy can readily be planned to deal with the occasional problems. But some of the deepest, most profound expectations may dwell in our subconscious minds and be much more difficult to articulate.

- As time goes on, some relationships get into deeper trouble. Of these expectations that have been gathering over the years, some may be profoundly disappointed. Most people have some sense that they want to try to work it out and find happiness and contentment in their situation. They want to try to figure out what's wrong, try talking through the problems, or do things to take a break from the stress that has been building over these troubled expectations. Sometimes there are strategies that seem to help temporarily. The relationship gets better for a while, then worse, then better and then worse.

- Assuming nothing happens to turn things around, usually one person makes a decision. They often don't tell anyone about it for some period of time. Nevertheless, the decision has been made; a separation will happen. Apparently, it just takes time to rationally process how and when to act on the decision. For some people, this may be a matter of weeks or months. For others, it may take years.

- At some point, it becomes time to act. This usually first involves informing the other party and other people around you. It is no longer a question of *if* the separation will occur, but rather *how* it will occur. Emotionally, it may get worse before it starts to get better.

- If a separation is to be as healthy as possible, new boundaries need to be negotiated and set to minimize the risk of ongoing problems.

- While you may feel like the relational wrangling is over, there may well be a small mountain of hurt, anger, grief, denial, depression, and other emotions that will need to be dealt with. It has been easier to address problems by blaming them on the past relationship. Now you have to take responsibility for yourself. The separation isn't *really* over until many of these painful emotions have been laid to rest.

So, what does it mean to end your relationship with food? For most of you, you are still in those stages of disappointed expectations. Every attempt at dieting is just one more attempt at making the relationship work. Regardless of which strategy you use, or how much motivation and will power you can muster, as long as you allow your relationship with food, you will continue to live with the hope of fixing this troubled relationship. In fact, giving a lot of time and attention to food by dieting may only serve to make you more enmeshed in your relationship with food. Things may get better for some period of time. There may well be occasions of happiness and contentment, perhaps a reasonable truce. Soon enough, it is so easy to go back to the *comfort food*. Your weight may have gone down some, but the relationship is as strong as ever. The relational issues are what you need to come to grips with if you want to address the root issue.

There are those of you who are currently taking a hard look in the mirror, realizing that you have arrived at that moment of decision. The relationship isn't working, and trying to fix it one more time by dieting isn't going to help in the long run. You are ready to step into that place where you know that you have made the decision; you just aren't sure how you're going to turn this decision into action. Have faith; you can do this.

Take a moment to look back. From the day you were born, food became a way by which you were connected to soothing, love, and intimacy. There are mountains of life experiences that have fostered your relationship with food. To stand on the threshold of this change means to move beyond a powerful relationship that has guided a million tiny actions in your life, mostly involving the movement of your hand toward your mouth. It is difficult to predict what the emotional turmoil will be for you as you move in this direction. Perhaps take a moment to reread the ramifications of other types of separation. Taking the steps necessary to separate yourself from your relationship with food may or may not be easy for you. Just the thought of letting go of their relationship with food has stirred up difficult emotions in people who are facing up to this.

Understand: food is just food, nothing more, nothing less.

Think for a moment about what you step on as you walk out of the building that you call home. For most of us, this pavement is concrete. We take it for granted. We clean it when it gets dirty. We shovel the snow off it when it gets covered. We appreciate it only in as much as it prevents the mud from getting on our shoes. If it was properly poured, it will last for many long years. Concrete is just concrete. This is not difficult to accept. Our expectations are disappointed only when the concrete crumbles. Most of us do not carry warm feelings of comfort about concrete.

Take a moment to think about the fact that food is just food. It cannot and never will be your comforter, lover, stress reliever, entertainer, or counselor. It is the series of chemical compounds that our bodies need to grow, survive, and thrive, no more, no less. To pile a bunch of meaning on to some smell, taste, texture, quantity, or quality of food is to anchor yourself in this relationship. It is great to enjoy food. You may well enjoy a nice stretch of concrete after having to walk through the mud, but it isn't likely that you're going to develop a relationship with the concrete. It's wonderful that you can gain some pleasure and satisfaction enjoying well-prepared food, as long as you remember that it's just food. It is great to enjoy the smell of fresh baked bread, but when you connect it too closely to your mother's love for you, you only foster your relationship with food, not with your mother.

So, if it's just food, it should be easy to simply stop thinking about food in relational terms and start thinking about it as just food, right? Well, maybe. Now is the time that you need to summon a portion of discipline. This discipline is important for what we will call the *food impulse*. It's any occasion like when you've had a good supper; your hunger has been satisfied, and there is no physiological or nutritional need that has not been fulfilled. Yet you find yourself with your hand on the refrigerator door, about to seek something more to eat. At this moment ask yourself, "What do I really need?"

Much of the potential help that you might get from this concept hinges on this one simple question asked at the right time. If you can take this opportunity to seriously consider what you might be needing at that point in time, you have a good chance of not only avoiding placing extra calories in your body that are not needed, but also finding fulfillment in a root area of your life where it is needed. Then for you to muster the courage to answer that question in the healthiest, most productive way possible is important. To ask and answer this question successfully on a regular basis will slowly change the nature of who you are.

"What do I really need?"

This is a good time for you to find a piece of paper. Write down a list of the most common occasions when you are most prone to eating for reasons other than hunger. Next to each item on this list, write the strategy that will work for you to remind you to ask this question. A sticky note on the door of the refrigerator might be a good place to start. Review the list before you go to a party or dinner with friends. This strategy will not work if you do not remember to ask the question.

Ask the question when you are considering a snack in the afternoon, when you're thinking about taking a second serving of your mama's lasagna, when someone brings food to the office, or when you're just wishing for a little something before you go to bed. What do you really need? If you are truly hungry, and your body needs nourishment, get the quantity and type of food to eat so that your body can be satisfied. But often it will occur to you that there is something else you need, such as comfort, relief from stress, or whatever. That is the point when you have to step up and attend to that very real emotional need. The more that you do this, the more quickly you will be able to identify the need and develop strategies for attending to it. Maturity is clearly identifying a need and taking the responsibility to attend to it. If you are lonely, talk to your spouse or a friend. Journaling works well for some people. The act of putting a strategy down on paper can be very helpful. You have spent a lot of years trying to solve difficult issues with a simple answer: putting food in your mouth. Now you need to be mature enough to deal with grown-up problems by coming up with grown-up solutions.

Asking this question is an important challenge, but developing plans for what you do once you've answered the question is equally as important. Again, if you are truly hungry, get something to eat. Be a little careful to not mistake thirst for hunger. If you are not sure, get some water to drink. It's not a bad idea to grab a glass of water every time you have an impulse to eat. Water is good for you! Then, if you still need something more, go for a satisfying snack. If you need stress relief, go for a walk or try some other type of exercise. Serious stress is often accompanied by an adrenalin surplus. Burn it off. If you feel like your world is filled with chaos and you need to get control of something, clean your kitchen or desk. (Hey, it works for me!) If you feel angry or guilty about something, take time to talk to someone. If you find that you regularly are dealing with depression, seek medical help. It's up to you to take responsibility for putting together the strategies that work for you. But they all hinge on your taking that half second to ask the question, "What do I really need?" Remember the mosaic mentioned earlier? These are the points where you will begin changing the bits of colors.

One person who took this approach, we will call her Alice, got in a regular habit of asking this question several times each day. She had been divorced for a number of years and considered herself to be rather independent and free-spirited. During the first weeks she was trying out this method, there were numerous occasions that she asked the question, "What do I really need?" It was surprising to her that often the answer came, "I'm lonely." She had just never considered herself a lonely person! Even during the quiet moments, she was never bored. Because she had asked the question often

A MISDIAGNOSED NATION | 301

enough and was serious about addressing the answers, she gained a whole new insight into an area of her life that needed attention. She had been successful in using this tool to restrain her overeating, but she had also found a way to open up a portion of her life where she had emotional needs that were going unfulfilled. As she learned the root cause of this impulse, she was able to work on a strategy to address the real need. Alice had spent a large part of her life struggling with loneliness, but each time it recurred for her, she reached out for food to fill the need. Now the task before her was to discover how this void in her life could be filled in a healthier way.

Even with all of this serious stuff, don't be too hard on yourself. You *never* want to focus too much on the food! Giving yourself permission to *walk outside the lines* now and then can take away a little of the emotional pressure to do things just right, or else you'll feel guilty about it for days. You don't have to get the right answer every single time. If you can get this right even 80 or 90 percent of the time, there will be huge improvements for you. Any strategy for taking better care of yourself where you end up spending a lot of time focusing on the food or beating yourself up because you didn't do it right will be self-defeating. It is important to be good to yourself. Food is just food.

There is a tangent that should be addressed at this point. What does a person do about cravings? This question does not have one simple answer. There may be several reasons mingled together. The first one is what I've just finished talking about: using food to meet an emotional need. It has become a learned reflex for you to go looking for *comfort food* when things go wrong. Another problem might be with the various forms of sugar. These can have biochemical roots. This would be another reason for you to visit your physician. Women often observe that cravings can occur when they have hormonal changes in their bodies. There is some evidence that we crave foods to which we have an intolerance. A group of chemicals that we call *chocolate* has a long list of potentially troublesome substances related to its makeup and the way it's grown, stored, and processed. Yet over time, the body will end up craving those very chemicals that are damaging to it. Cravings may also be induced by sounds, smells, and any number of visual or cognitive events. If you are particularly cursed by cravings that may be intolerance-related, don't be shy about seeing your doctor or an allergy specialist. Do not simply cave in to a craving and then get angry with yourself when you stumble. Do a little research to find out what the origin of the craving is and how you can deal with it.

Recognize that there are three key elements to effectively use this strategy:

1. Remember to ask the question: "What do I really need?"

2. Take a moment to look at the answers that come to you.

3. Choose from the array of options as to which is the best, healthiest choice through which the need might be met. To achieve this, you will

need to engrain in yourself the habits necessary to do this. A few people are going to pick up this idea, and do it.

Perhaps the best way to go at this is to take a period of time during which you will keep a journal. This will be totally unlike the food journaling you may have done before. You will not spend any time focusing on the food. The point is to make an entry in your journal every time you have a *food impulse* of any kind. If you wake up in the morning and feel hungry, write about how hungry you are and how active you will be through the morning. Tell how it helps you decide how much to eat. Give yourself permission to eat the amount of food that will get you through the morning. Later in the day, if you have a *food impulse*, ask the question, "What do I really need?" If you sense one or more emotional needs at that moment, write down what they are and all of the options that come to mind for addressing each need. You may be very surprised over the course of the first several days as you do this. You may find several recurring needs, some of which you may not have been aware of. If you can, make a serious effort in doing this. Find a certain number of days that you can commit to. Do not let it become drudgery. Even though there is a little work involved, do it as long as you feel you are getting something out of it. Journaling for less than four days probably will not be very valuable. Seven days will generally get you off to a good start. For those of you who enjoy journaling, six weeks or more can be a great opportunity to explore this process of ending your relationship with food.

Here is another approach you can take that can help you reinforce the important steps: draw out a chart that you can put up on your refrigerator or some other visible place. Make this chart so that it has an item for every possible reason you might have an impulse to eat. It will be good if you can include a little artwork to go with each item. Whenever you have an impulse to eat, literally place your finger on that location on the chart which best describes the underlying reason. Pause for a moment to consider your options. This is a worthwhile mechanism to use over the course of the first couple of months that you use this strategy.

It is also a good idea to take a little time every week to reflect on how your relationship with food is changing. Be intentional enough about it so that you either write in your journal or set aside time to talk with a supportive friend about how you see changes. Best of all, find a friend with whom you can walk through this whole process together. Every journey is better when taken with a friend.

Anyone who knows anything about weight loss talks about both diet and exercise. Hopefully, you've got the message that food is just food. It is there to provide for the biochemical needs of your body, not for your relational needs. Perhaps it would be a good idea to come at exercise with a similar approach. Don't exercise just to lose weight. Exercise because it is good for you in many different ways. It can be enjoyable, relieves stress, and helps you grow stronger and more capable. All of the benefits that we are considering are compounded when you can enjoy exercising. The point in all of this is to do what you enjoy and what brings you the greatest amount of fulfillment.

Whatever you do, don't start out by training for the Olympics. You'll end up miserable. Walking is wonderful. So are swimming and bicycling. Choose activities that aren't hard on your joints. If you are exercising and are breathing so hard you can't talk, you're working too hard. If you work out for a few days, and your muscles are getting more than a little sore, you need to back off. Don't make this drudgery. Find the kind of exercise that is most enjoyable, and you will keep doing it. Better yet, find a friend or group of friends who will join you in the venture. The exercise and activities you love will add even more bits of color to your mosaic.

If you are uncertain how any level of exercise may affect you, consult a doctor. They may be able to point you to some literature that gets you started exercising in ways that are appropriate for your age and build.

As you can see, the reasons we eat have to do with habits, hunger, and thirst. The reasons we overeat often have to do with our emotional and relational needs. Tragically, a sad mistake we make is when we beat ourselves up because we've *blown* our diet. Again, anything that leads us to focus on the food is self-defeating. Food is just food. What you ate over the past five or ten days should have no meaning to you now. If there is a little extra food hanging around your stomach because your last meal was too large, let that inform you how and when you eat your next meal. Keep this simple. At any time you are anxious about it, just ask the question, "What do I really need?" To hang on to guilt or shame on past occasions when you ate more than you needed just draws you back into that old relationship with food. It does you no good. The past is in the past.

Perhaps you are choosing to end your relationship with food. If you've ever been close to a relationship that's fallen apart, or gone through one yourself, you know that it can be a long and involved process. Some of the steps can be difficult or painful. The secret to coming through it is not in avoiding the difficulty or pain. Rather it is in walking through the pain, bit by bit, step by step. Some of the most important spiritual journeys we experience in life involve moving from bondage to freedom, from guilt to forgiveness, from despair to hope. If moving through this process unearths past experiences that are traumatic or abusive, do not hesitate to seek someone for professional help. Happiness and fulfillment await you. You can do this.

This venture truly is unburdening. You will literally watch the pounds go away. But just as importantly, you will be changing the colors that make up the portrait of who you are. This is not because you are more slender! It is because you have taken the responsibility at certain moments in time to ask the question, "What do I really need?" You have stepped up to look for the best possible answer. This will not happen overnight. But as the first weeks and months go by, you will see change. The benefits of this will touch every aspect of your life. Using this strategy will not require an abundance of willpower, but it may require substantial courage.

As you find you are getting certain answers back from your persistent questioning, it will require that you do more than just assemble the options that seem obvious. It may involve creating a whole new set of intentions for having these needs met. Remember, you have spent a lifetime turning to your relationship with food to have certain needs met. Now is the time to deal with these needs directly. Do not hesitate to seek professional counseling if you anticipate walking into some tough, unresolved issues in your life. Think again for a moment of this mosaic portrait you have of yourself. Zoom out a little to see that it involves much more than just a snapshot of you and your body. It encompasses a wide range of your hopes, dreams, and relationships. While you have maintained this relationship with food, a substantial portion of the portrait got taken up with that one relationship. In coming months, you face this prospect of, bit by bit, shrinking that down to the point where food is no more than something in the background. That will be the point where food is just food. That is when you face a really exciting possibility. Once you remove the space in your life that was filled with your relationship with food, with what will you refill that space? What might you do in your relationship with yourself? Are there service or educational interests that you've wished to pursue? Perhaps your relationships with your spouse, children, friends, or family members have room for improvement.

As I've introduced this concept to different individuals and groups and chatted about their struggles with weight loss, I've received a number of excellent questions. Here are several questions and responses which may be helpful to you.

Question: Would it make sense to first do a diet plan that I know will get me down to the weight I wish to be, *then* adopt this strategy?

While you might think this is possible, I haven't found it very workable. Imagine doing a three-month diet where you spend a lot of time focusing on what and how much you are going to eat. At the end of this, you switch to telling yourself to stop focusing on the food and start focusing on your relational needs that queue your desire to eat. You will be doing this at the same time your body is transitioning out of *famine mode*. These may not be easy transitions for you to make. The focus of each of these efforts may be very different.

Incidentally, there are a number of techniques put forward by diet plans that are helpful. Eat more slowly; it gives your body more time to feel satisfied as you eat. (This may be one of the key reasons Europeans, for example, are much less prone to obesity than Americans.) Take lots of opportunities to drink water. Make a point of eating until you are no longer hungry rather than eating until you are full. While these are a few tricks that can be very helpful, don't get caught up in them so much that you spend all your time focusing on the food.

Question: I have these deeply engrained connections between food and my family relationships. To consider ending these connections, it feels like I'd be cutting off a part of myself. What if I'm not ready to do that?

Don't do something that you are not ready to do. Rather than make a big decision about how you are going to proceed with this strategy, take some time to step back and ponder how this relationship with food is working for you. Separate it into two questions: How are my relationships with friends and family members working? (And what do I need to do about them?) How is my relationship with food working? The more cleanly you can separate these two questions, the sooner you will arrive at the healthiest possible answers.

Question: I love the holidays and other celebrations, with all of the great food and treats being passed around. How do I deal with all of that?

The holidays do put in front of you a lot of opportunities to respond to old impulses. When you have a relationship with food, the act of eating and celebrating with friends and family are so interconnected that there is no separating the two. The trick is to focus on the healthy relationships with friends and family. You can still eat; just don't put away fourteen of Aunt Nellie's Christmas cookies for hors d'oeuvres. Celebrating with loved ones and eating don't have to be connected. Enjoy plenty of the intimacy with a little less of the food.

Question: Just like I did when I used to diet, I cave in, eat too much, and end up feeling guilty about everything that I've just eaten. How do I get past this?

As the saying goes, guilt is the gift that keeps on giving. Rather than letting guilt pile up, ask what it will take to get better at forgiving yourself for whatever mistakes you have made. Forgiveness can be a powerful force. Once you have dealt with residual guilt, don't be too hard on yourself. Gain confidence that, in the long run, your body is generally going to be moving toward its ideal weight, so any slip-ups or overzealous celebrations are only incidental detours on your path. Don't beat yourself up. To carry a lot of guilt over eating means that you are moving back toward your relationship with food, which becomes self-defeating.

Question: I ask myself the question, "What do I really need?" but how do I trust the answer?

First, are you asking this question on a regular basis? If you only ask it every now and then, it will be harder for you to become aware of how you are relating to food. Most of the time people are pretty good about being honest with themselves. You aren't dealing with a seventh grader who will lie to get out of a tight spot. With many folks, the answers are usually fairly obvious, and the task that requires more discipline is evaluating the range of choices with which to respond to that particular need. If you find that you are uncertain or confused by your answer, it may mean that there is more than one need presenting itself. You may want to give some additional thought to evaluating your choices as you proceed.

Question: Is it possible that I will ever be at a point where I have completely ended my relationship with food and won't have to think about it anymore?

It is likely going to be like any relationship. If you have just been casual friends with food, seeking little more than periodic distractions, you may be able to move on quickly and easily. But for those who have had a very close, lifelong, intimate relationship, where you have regularly turned to this *lover* as you felt some perceived need, it may be more difficult. Think about the person who has ended a long marriage through a bitter divorce. A long and intentional healing process is necessary, with some likelihood that the frustration will never be 100 percent resolved. It is best to not think of it as a destination to be arrived at, but rather an important journey to be ventured.

Question: Would it be true that individuals who struggle with their weight have greater emotional problems than other people?

While it may be true that there is emotional strain on an overweight person caused by their obesity, every person has an array of relational, emotional, and spiritual needs. The difference is that some people have shunted these needs toward their relationship with food. Every person grows up developing ways of addressing these needs. Some approaches are profoundly healthier than others. I hope this chapter of the book has helped you think about the root issue under that extra few pounds and find a healthier solution to that root issue.

ENDNOTES

Chapter 1 – Diagnosing Life's Issues

1.   "Virtually No Change in Annual Harris Poll Confidence Index from Last Year," Harris Interactive, dated March 9, 2010, http://www.harrisinteractive.com/NewsRoom/HarrisPolls/tabid/447/ctl/ReadCustom%20Default/mid/1508/ArticleId/232/Default.aspx.

Chapter 2 – The Root Pyramids

2.   "The Holocaust," History Learning Site, last accessed January 12, 2012, http://www.historylearningsite.co.uk/holocaust.htm.

3.   "$160 Million Spent on Negative Political Ads," Politics on MSNBC.com, dated November 2, 2006, http://www.msnbc.msn.com/id/15495778/ns/politics/t/million-spent-negative-political-ads.

Chapter 3 – Case Study #1: The Root Cause of Obesity

4.   "Prevalence of overweight, obesity and extreme obesity among adults: United States, trends 1976-80 through 2005-2006," NHCS Health E-Stats, December 2008, http://www.cdc.gov/nchs/data/hestat/overweight/overweight_adult.pdf, p. 4.

5.   "Prevalence of Individual Adverse Childhood Experiences," Centers for Disease Control and Prevention, dated September 20, 2010, http://cdc.gov/ace/prevalence.htm.

6.   "Body weight and obesity in adults and self-reported abuse in childhood," Pubmed.gov, dated August 26, 2002, http://www.ncbi.nlm.nih.gov/pubmed/12119573.

7.   "Prevalence of Individual Adverse Childhood Experiences," Centers for Disease Control and Prevention, dated September 20, 2010, http://cdc.gov/ace/prevalence.htm.

8.   "Weight-loss help: Gain control of emotional eating," MayoClinic.com, dated December 1, 2009, www.mayoclinic.com/health/weight-loss/MH00025/METHOD=print.

Chapter 4 – Case Study #2:
The Root Cause of Crime

9.   Kumpfer, Karol L., and Alvarado, Rose, "Family-Strengthening Approaches for the Prevention of Youth Problem Behaviors," *American Psychologist*, June/July, 2003, p. 457.

10.   Kumpfer, Karol L., and Alvarado, Rose, "Family-Strengthening Approaches for the Prevention of Youth Problem Behaviors," *American Psychologist*, June/July, 2003, p. 457.

11.   "Re-entry Trends in the U.S.," Bureau of Justice Statistics, last revised June 30, 2011, http://bjs.ojp.usdoj.gov/content/reentry/recidivism.cfm.

12.   "All Children Excel (ACE) Executive Summary," Preliminary Outcome Evaluation Study, dated January 2002, p. 3.

13.   "Morgan Quitno's 13th Annual Safest (and Most Dangerous) Cities," last accessed June 30, 2011, http://www.morganquitno.com/cit07pop.htm#25.

14.   Addressing Child Trauma in Juvenile Justice and Residential Settings," Child Welfare League of America, The Link, Spring 2005, http://www.cwla.org/programs/juvenilejustice/thelink2005spring.pdf, p. 8.

15.   Merriam-Webster's Collegiate Dictionary, Eleventh Edition, Merriam-Webster Incorporated, 2004.

16.   "Can Married Parents Prevent Crime"? Institute for Marriage and Public Policy (iMAPP), September 21, 2005, http://www.marriagedebate.com/pdf/imapp.crimefamstructure.pdf, p. 1.

17.   "America's Children: Key National Indicators of Well-Being, 2009," Federal Interagency Forum on Child and Family Statistics, last accessed June 28, 2011, http://www.childstats.gov/pdf/ac2009/ac_09.pdf, p. 14.

18.   "Adverse Childhood Experiences (ACE) Major Findings," Centers for Disease & Prevention, September 20, 2010, http://cdc.gov/ace/findings.htm.

19.   "Prevalence of Individual Adverse Childhood Experiences," Centers for Disease & Prevention, dated September 20, 2010, http://cdc.gov/ace/prevalence.htm.

20.   "Adverse Childhood Experiences (ACE) Major Findings," Centers for Disease & Prevention, September 20, 2010, http://cdc.gov/ace/findings.htm.

21.   "Courts & Corrections," State Budget Solutions, last accessed June 30, 2011, http://www.statebudgetsolutions.org/issues/detail/courts-corrections.

22.   "Changing Patterns of Nonmarital Childbearing in the United States," NCHS Data Brief, May 2009, http://www.cdc.gov/nchs/data/databriefs/db18.htm.

23.   "Changing Patterns of Nonmarital Childbearing in the United States," NCHS Data Brief, dated May 2009, http://www.cdc.gov/nchs/data/databriefs/db18.htm.

24.   "National Health Expenditure Data," Centers for Medicare and Medicaid Services, last revised June 20, 2011, https://www.cms.gov/nationalhealthexpend-data/02_nationalhealthaccountshistorical.asp.

25.   "Nationally Representative CDC Study Finds 1 in 4 Teenage Girls Has a Sexually Transmitted Disease," Centers for Disease and Prevention, March 11, 2008, http://www.cdc.gov/stdconference/2008/press/release-11march2008.htm.

26.   "Trends in the Elderly Population," Aging in the Know, The AGS Foundation for Health in Aging, last accessed June 30, 2011, http://www.healthinaging.org/agingintheknow/chapters_ch_trial.asp?ch=2.

27.   "The World Factbook," Central Intelligence Agency, last accessed June 22, 2011, https://www.cia.gov/library/publications/the-world-factbook/geos/us.html.

28.   "Using the web as a weapon: The internet as a tool for violent radicalization and homegrown terrorism," Hearing before the Subcommittee on intelligence, information sharing, and terrorism risk assessment of the Committee on Homeland Security, House of Representatives, dated November 6, 2007, http://www.fas.org/irp/congress/2007_hr/web.pdf.

29.   "Giving U.S.A Featured in the Media," Giving U.S.A, June 30, 2010, http://www.usatoday.com/yourlife/mind-soul/doing-good/2010-11-29-sharing-by-the-numbers-graphic_N.htm.

30.   "Adverse Childhood Experiences (ACE) Major Findings," Centers for Disease & Prevention, September 20, 2010, http://cdc.gov/ace/findings.htm.

31. "Kumpfer, Karol L., and Alvarado, Rose, "Family-Strengthening Approaches for the Prevention of Youth Problem Behaviors," American Psychologist, June/July, 2003, p. 457.

32. "Teenage Sexual Abstinence and Academic Achievement," The Heritage Foundation, dated August 2005, http://www.heritage.org/Research/Reports/2005/10/Teenage-Sexual-Abstinence-and-Academic-Achievement.

33. "Adverse Childhood Experiences (ACE) Major Findings," Centers for Disease & Prevention, September 20, 2010, http://cdc.gov/ace/findings.htm.

34. "I Need a Father (a father's role in child custody)," Texas Department of Corrections, dated October 2010, http://www.fathersrightsdallas.com/tag/texas-dept-of-corrections.

35. "Mentoring Does Work," Pew Public/Private Ventures Study, Be A Mentor website, http://www.beamentor.org/taxdeductible_2.htm.

Chapter 5 – Case Study #3:
A Root Cause of a Root Cause of Crime

36. "Fetal Alcohol Syndrome: Diagnosis, Epidemiology, Prevention, and Treatment" (1996) Institute of Medicine (IOM), Page 35 http://books.nap.edu/openbook.php?record_id=4991&page=35

37. "Getting an Early Start on Fetal Alcohol Spectrum Disorders," Dr. Larry Burd, Department of Pediatrics, FAS Clinic, University of North Dakota, http://eclkc.ohs.acf.hhs.gov/hslc/tta-system/ehsnrc/Early%20Head%20Start/early-learning/disabilities/Getting%20an%20Early%20Start%20on%20Fetal%20Alcohol%20Spectrum%20Disorders.htm

38. "On Big Isle, fetal drug and alcohol exposure wide-spread," West Hawaii Today, http://www.westhawaiito-day.com/sections/news/local-news/big-isle-fetal-drug-and-alcohol-exposure-widespread.html

39. Streissguth, Ann, Fetal Alcohol Syndrome, University of Washington School of Medicine. Paul H. Brookes Publishing Co., pp. 23-27.

40. Streissguth, A.P.; Aase, J.M.; Clarren, S.K.; Randels, S.P.; LaDue, R.A.; Smith, D.F. "Fetal Alcohol Syndrome in Adolescents and Adults," *Journal of the American Medical Association,* 1991, pp. 265:1961-1967.

   Mattson, S.N.; Riley, E.P.; Gramling, L.; Delis, D.C.; Jones, K.L., "Heavy Prenatal Alcohol Exposure With or Without Physical Features of Fetal Alcohol Syndrome Leads to IQ Deficits. Journal of Pediatrics, 1997, pp. 131 (5), 718-721.

   Mattson, S.N.; Riley, E.P; "A Review of the Neurobehavioral Deficits in Children with Fetal Alcohol Syndrome or Prenatal exposure to Alcohol," Alcoholism: Clinical and Experimental Research, 1998, pp. 22 (2), 279-294.

41. Eyal, Roy, "Psychiatric Training in Fetal Alcohol Spectrum Disorders Inadequate," Semel Institute for Neuroscience & Human Behavior at the University of California–Los Angeles, American Academy of Child & Adolescent Psychiatry, 56th Annual Meeting: Abstract 2.20. Presented October 29, 2009.

42. "Taking a Closer Look; Drinking During Pregnancy in Minnesota," MN Dept. of Health, Market Street Research, Inc., 2002.

43. "Fetal Alcohol Syndrome Research," International Adoption Project-IAP, http://www.med.umn.edu/peds/iac/research/fas/home.html

44. Streissguth, Ann, Fetal Alcohol Syndrome, University of Washington School of Medicine. Paul H. Brookes Publishing Co., pp. 102-103.

45. Streissguth, Ann, Fetal Alcohol Syndrome, University of Washington School of Medicine. Paul H. Brookes Publishing Co., pp. 104-111.

46. Burd, Larry; Selfridge, Rachael H.; Klug, Marilyn G.; Juelson, Tim; "Fetal Alcohol Syndrome in the Canadian Corrections System," 2003, pp. 1:e14

47. Hetland, Cara; Robertson, Tom, "Fetal Alcohol Syndrome: The Invisible Disorder," Minnesota Public Radio, September 6, 2007.

48. "Annual Report on the Public Debt: Fiscal Year Ending on September 30, 2010," Department of the Treasury, June 2011, http://waysandmeans.house.gov/UploadedFiles/FY2010_ANNUAL_REPORT.pdf.

Chapter 6 – The Root Cause of the National Debt

49. "Chinese Plants Grow on U.S. Turf," *Bloomberg Businessweek*, January 3-9, 2011, pp. 425-432.

50. "The Public's Opinions on Congress: Q & A with Center Research Director Carmines," The Center on Congress at Indiana University, March 14, 2011, http://congress.indiana.edu/the-public%E2%80%99s-opinions-congress-q-center-research-director-carmines.

51. "Annual Report on the Public Debt: Fiscal Year Ending on September 30, 2010," Department of the Treasury, June 2011, http://waysandmeans.house.gov/UploadedFiles/FY2010_ANNUAL_REPORT.pdf.

52. Cayton, Andrew; Perry Elisabeth Israels; Reed, Linds; Winkler, Allan M., *America: Pathways to the Present*, Pearson Prentice Hall, 2003, p. 414.

53. "The Gettysburg Address," Abraham Lincoln, http://www.gettysburgaddress.com/HTMLS/ga.html.

Chapter 7 – A Better Diagnosis

54. "Changing Patterns of Nonmarital Childbearing in the United States," NCHS Data Brief, Number 18, May 2009, http://www.cdc.gov/nchs/data/databriefs/db18.htm.

55. "Facts About Obesity in the United States," Centers for Disease Control and Prevention website, last accessed June 28, 2011, http://www.cdc.gov/PDF/Facts_About_Obesity_in_the_United_States.pdf.

56. "Table S-4. Proposed Budget by Category," OMB 2012 Budget, http://www.whitehouse.gov/sites/default/files/omb/budget/fy2012/assets/tables.pdf, p. 176.

57. "Table S-4. Proposed Budget by Category," OMB 2012 Budget, http://www.whitehouse.gov/sites/default/files/omb/budget/fy2012/assets/tables.pdf, p. 176.

58. "Table S-4. Proposed Budget by Category," OMB 2012 Budget, http://www.whitehouse.gov/sites/default/files/omb/budget/fy2012/assets/tables.pdf, p. 176.

59. GAO Alternative Scenario, U.S. Government Accountability Office, http://www.gao.gov/special.pubs/longterm/fall2009_alttrustees.pdf. [2021 GAO alternate scenario x OMB Debt Held by the Public (Table S-4. Proposed Budget by Category," OMB 2012 Budget)]

60. Carson, Clarence B, "George Washington's Farewell Address," *Basic American Government*, American Textbook Committee, 2001, p. 561-562.

61. Merriam-Webster's Collegiate Dictionary, Eleventh Edition, Merriam-Webster Incorporated, 2004.

62. "Changing Patterns of Nonmarital Childbearing in the United States," NCHS Data Brief, Number 18, May 2009, http://www.cdc.gov/nchs/data/databriefs/db18.htm.

63. Ranier, Thom S.; Rainer, Jess W., The Millennials: Connecting to America's Largest Generation, B & H Books, Nashville, TN, 2011.

64. "Young Mississippians: Ready, Willing, and Unable to Serve," Mission: Readiness, Military Leaders for Kids, 2009, http://www.missionreadiness.org/PAEE0609.pdf, p. 6.

65. Rubenzer, Steven J., Faschingbauer, Thomas R., Ones, Deniz S., "Assessing the U.S. Presidents Using the Revised Neo Personality Inventory," (Volume 7, Number 4), pp. 403-420, copyright © 2000 by Psychological Assessment Resources, Inc., Reprinted by Permission of Sage Publications.

Chapter 8 – The Root of a Leader

66. "Virtually No Change in Annual Harris Poll Confidence Index from Last Year," dated March 9, 2010, http://www.harrisinteractive.com/NewsRoom/HarrisPolls/tabid/447/ctl/ReadCustom%20Default/mid/1508/ArticleId/232/Default.aspx.

67. "Samuel Adams Quotes," taken from Samuel Adam's letter to James Warren, November 4, 1775, http://www.revolutionary-war-and-beyond.com/samuel-adams-quotes-1.html.

68. Barton, David, Original Intent, Wallbuilder Press, Aledo, TX, 2000, p. 348.

69. "Winzenburg (name now changed to Kiley), Vanessa, "Maximize Your Leadership Potential," *FMI Quarterly*, Issue 3, 2008, p. 24-28.

Chapter 9 – The Solutions

70. "Program Assessment: Mentoring Children of Prisoners," ExpectMore.gov, http://georgewbush-whitehouse.archives.gov/omb/expectmore/summary/10003505.2005.html.

71. Deming, W. Edwards, "The New Economics," Massachusetts Institute of Technology, Center for Advanced Educational Services, Cambridge, Massachusetts, 1994, p. 132.

72. "Virtually No Change in Annual Harris Poll Confidence Index from Last Year," Harris Interactive, dated March 9, 2010, http://www.harrisinteractive.com/NewsRoom/HarrisPolls/tabid/447/ctl/ReadCustom%20Default/mid/1508/ArticleId/232/Default.aspx.

73. "Declaration of Independence," The Charters of Freedom, http://www.archives.gov/exhibits/charters/declaration_transcript.html.

74. "Concord Coalition," http://www.concordcoalition.org/.

75. "Red Ink Rising," Peterson-Pew Commission on Budget Reform, December 2009, http://budgetreform.org/sites/default/files/Red_Ink_Rising.pdf.

Chapter 10 – The Summary

76. "Declaration of Independence," The Charters of Freedom, http://www.archives.gov/exhibits/charters/declaration_transcript.html.

77.   Carson, Clarence B., *Basic American Government*, American Textbook Committee, 2001, p. 77.

78.   Blackstone, Sir William, "Commentaries on the Laws of England," The Laws of Nature and Nature's God, http://www.lonang.com/exlibris/blackstone/bla-002.htm.

79.   Cashman, Kevin, *Leadership from the Inside Out*, 2nd Edition, Berrett-Koehler Publishers, Inc., p. 35.

80.   Northouse, Peter, *Leadership: Theory and Practice*, 5th Edition, Sage Publishing, 2010, p. 171.

81.   Cashman, Kevin, *Leadership from the Inside Out*, 2nd Edition, Berrett-Koehler Publishers, Inc., p. 189.

82.   Northouse, Peter, *Leadership: Theory and Practice*, 5th Edition, Sage Publishing, 2010, p. 172.

83.   Kreitner, Robert; Kinicki, Angelo; *Organizational Leadership*, 9th Edition, McGraw-Hill/Irwin, 2010, p. 485.

84.   Carson, Clarence B, "George Washington's Farewell Address," *Basic American Government*, American Textbook Committee, 2001, p. 561-562.

85.   Barton, David, *Original Intent*, Wallbuilder Press, Aledo, TX, 2000, p. 319.

86.   Barton, David, *Original Intent*, Wallbuilder Press, Aledo, TX, 2000, p. 226.

87.   Barton, David, *Original Intent*, Wallbuilder Press, Aledo, TX, 2000, p. 320.

88.   Barton, David, *Original Intent*, Wallbuilder Press, Aledo, TX, 2000, p. 320.

89.   Barton, David, *Original Intent*, Wallbuilder Press, Aledo, TX, 2000, p. 321.

90. "About: Mission Statement," The Salvation Army, last accessed January, 7, 2012, http://www.salvationarmyusa.org/usn/www_usn_2.nsf/vw-local/About-us.

91. Barton, David, *Original Intent*, Wallbuilder Press, Aledo, TX, 2000, p. 213.

92. "Table 1348. Gross National Income (GNI) by Country: 2000 and 2009," U.S. Census Bureau, last accessed January 12, 2012, http://www.census.gov/compendia/statab/2012/tables/12s1348.pdf.

93. Carson, Clarence B, "George Washington's Farewell Address," *Basic American Government*, American Textbook Committee, 2001, p. 561-562.

94. Genesis 1:24-26 (New King James Version)

95. Genesis 1:27 (New King James Version)

96. Kreitner, Robert; Kinicki, Angelo; *Organizational Leadership*, 9th Edition, McGraw-Hill/Irwin, 2010, p. 486.

97. James 4:10 (NKJV)

98. Matthew 6:33 (NKJV)

99. 2 Chronicles 7:14 (NKJV)

Appendix

100. "The High/Scope Perry Preschool Project," OJJDP Juvenile Justice Bulletin, October 2000, http://www.ncjrs.gov/pdffiles1/ojjdp/181725.pdf.

101. "Every Child Every Promise: Turning Failure Into Action," America's Promise Alliance, http://www.americaspromise.org/Resources/Research-and-Reports/~/media/Files/About/ECEP%20-%20Full%20Report.ashx.

102. "Juvenile Arrests 2006," OJJDP, Juvenile Justice Bulletin, November 2008, http://www.ncjrs.gov/pdffiles1/ojjdp/221338.pdf.

103. "Nationally Representative CDC Study Finds 1 in 4 Teenage Girls Has a Sexually Transmitted Disease," Center for Disease Control and Prevention, March 11, 2008, http://www.cdc.gov/stdconference/2008/press/release-11march2008.htm.

104. "Information Brief," Minnesota House of Representatives, Research Department, August 1999, http://www.house.leg.state.mn.us/hrd/pubs/costcrime.pdf, p. 10.

105. Rector, Robert, "The Size and Scope Of Means-Tested Welfare Spending," The Heritage Foundation, August 1, 2001, http://www.heritage.org/Research/Testimony/The-Size-and-Scope-Of-Means-Tested-Welfare-Spending.

106. Rector, Robert, "The Size and Scope Of Means-Tested Welfare Spending," The Heritage Foundation, August 1, 2001, http://www.heritage.org/Research/Testimony/The-Size-and-Scope-Of-Means-Tested-Welfare-Spending.

107. "Key Facts at a Glance," Bureau of Justice Statistics, last revised July 2, 2011, http://bjs.ojp.usdoj.gov/content/glance/corr2.cfm.

108. "Profile of Jail Inmates, 2002," Bureau of Justice Statistics Special Report, last accessed June 30, 2011, http://bjs.ojp.usdoj.gov/content/pub/pdf/pji02.pdf.

ROOT LESSON FROM THE BOOK:
Inwardly Sound & Outwardly Focused

Please visit us at
www.amisdiagnosednation.com